T0381017

Spiritual
Connection Within

How to Connect with God
through Effectual Prayers

W. Ruben Exantus

authorHOUSE®

AuthorHouse™
1663 Liberty Drive
Bloomington, IN 47403
www.authorhouse.com
Phone: 833-262-8899

Published by AuthorHouse 09/06/2023

ISBN: 979-8-8230-1408-3 (sc)
ISBN: 979-8-8230-1407-6 (e)

Library of Congress Control Number: 2023916883

Print information available on the last page.

Any people depicted in stock imagery provided by Getty Images are models, and such images are being used for illustrative purposes only. Certain stock imagery © *Getty Images.*

This book is printed on acid-free paper.

Scripture quotations marked NLT are taken from the Holy Bible, New Living Translation, copyright © *1996, 2004, 2007. Used by permission of Tyndale House Publishers, Inc. Carol Stream, Illinois 60188. All rights reserved. Website*

I dedicate this book to God the Father, the Son, and the Holy Spirit as one person who simultaneously listens, intercedes, and helps me to pray.

And to my friends, family, colleagues, and all believers who pray without ceasing!

Contents

A Note from the Author...ix

Acknowledgments xi

About the Author xiii

Introduction...xv

Chapter 1   Praying according to God's Will 1

Chapter 2   The Mystery of Prayer..9

Chapter 3   What Should We Pray For?...12

Chapter 4   Biblical Models of Prayer 30

Chapter 5   Praying with the Right Motivation 34

Chapter 6   Hindrances to Payer..37

Chapter 7   Pray with Thanksgiving 40

Chapter 8   Pray with Persistence...42

Chapter 9   Pray with Total Reliance on God 46

Chapter 10 Pray Systematically 52

Chapter 11 Why Does God Want Believers to Pray? 54

Chapter 12 Myths about Prayer.. 64

Chapter 13 Prayer and Biblical Fasting..72

Chapter 14 The Impact of Prayer..77

Chapter 15 Praying for Change...83

Chapter 16 Praying the Promises of God.......................................86

Chapter 17 My Prayers for You 90

Bibliography.. 101

From the Same Author 103

How to Develop Your Prayer Life.. 105

A Note from the Author

A few words about the origin of this book and why it was written will help the reader to understand its teaching. This book is the outcome of a series of Bible studies I taught on prayer at Grace Baptist Church of Apopka, a church I pastored for nearly twelve years in Orlando, Florida. The idea came to me while putting into practice what I taught the congregation concerning prayer according to God's will.

A great number of people go to church every week across America and around the world, but unfortunately, many never have a personal time with God in prayer. The only time they spend in prayer is when they gather with the congregation for corporate worship. Can you imagine a Christian who only prays to God once or twice a week? Prayers addressed with others practically means there is nothing personal about it. Don't get me wrong. I believe in corporate prayer, and I think it creates an atmosphere of worship and fellowship where many believers get together to pray. It is essential to the life of a church. The true church of God will not go without it. In addition, there are those who pray to God often and alone. They seek times of silence in their lives to be with God alone and pray. However, there is an important question that must be addressed if we want God to answer our prayers. Do we pray according to God's will? I believe deep in my heart that there is a great misinterpretation among Christians in regard to the subject of prayer, which leads to a lack of spiritual power in many followers of God. I think it's time for you to find out what might be the cause of that spiritual weakness.

Acknowledgments

I would like to express my gratitude to the many people who, one way or another, saw me through this book, including all friends and family who provided support, proofread, offered comments, and assisted in the editing and design.

I want to thank my wife, Florence, who supported and encouraged me to write this book. This was a long and difficult journey.

Lastly, I ask forgiveness of all those who have helped me over the years whose names I have failed to mention. I'm grateful to you as well.

About the Author

W. Ruben Exantus is a pastor, author, and spiritual leader. Most of his work has been devoted to providing nurture and guidance to Christians of all stages of life in the Christian faith. He has served numerous Christian organizations and nonprofits in the United States of America and abroad. He holds degrees in engineering and theology and a PhD in organizational management with a specialty in leadership. Dr. Exantus is a scholar-practitioner in the field of spiritual leadership with certifications in clinical pastoral education (CPE). He has written several books and articles, primarily focusing on leadership and ethics. Titles include *Pastoral Burnout and Leadership Styles: Factors Contributing to Stress and Ministerial Turnover*; *Ethics and Church Leadership*; *Pastoral Burnout and Leadership Styles: A Mixed Method Study of Southern Pastors in Central Florida*; and *Six Steps to Avoiding Hospice Work Burnout*. His books are available in all major bookstores in the United States.

Introduction

Praying effectively is praying according to the will of God.

We all need to learn how to communicate with God effectively. Communication is a skill that one must learn to exchange information. If we want to communicate with our creator, we must learn how to pray, which is the only communicative language that Christians have at their disposal to speak with God. Prayer is the way we communicate with God who created us and saved us through His Son, Jesus. Because God desires to be in a relationship with man, He speaks to us through His Word and the Holy Spirit who is in us who believe. God, through His Spirit, helps us understand His Word and apply it to our lives. For this to happen, we need to communicate back to God. It is through the means of prayer that we communicate back to God.

Christians should learn how to pray effectively. And we should model our prayer life on Jesus, the greatest teacher who ever walked this earth. We learned how to pray from our Lord, for He taught His disciples how to pray. Jesus's disciples noticed His prayerfulness and asked Him to teach them how to pray (Luke 11:1). They wanted to pray like John had taught his disciples. So Jesus did teach them how to pray.

I think it is safe to say that there is a learning curve in prayer, especially if you are a new believer in Jesus Christ. Many Christians think they already know how to pray. Therefore, teaching about prayer is not something they think is necessary. If everyone knows how to pray, why would there still be a need to teach how to pray? Well, I think there is indeed a need to be taught how to pray. You might say prayer seems a simple thing to do. After all, praying is communicating with God. As simple as this may sound, I must tell you that prayer is one of the most complex things we do as we walk with the Lord. While prayer may be complex, it doesn't have to be complicated. If something is complex, it means that it has many components. Complexity does not necessarily suggest difficulty. I'm speaking as an engineer who has resolved many complexed problems throughout my life. I'm familiar with complex issues. Something that is complex may not be as difficult as one may think. Complicated, on the other hand, refers to a high level of difficulty. If something is complicated, there might be or might not be many parts in it, but it will certainly take a lot of hard work to resolve. Theologically, one might say that prayer engages a person into some deep feeling, but it doesn't have to be a complicated and difficult practice for Christians. The reason is because prayer is something any believer can do anywhere at any time.

However, prayer is a science. You might say, "Why is prayer a science?" Let me explain. Anything that involves teaching involves knowledge. There has been a lot of debate about science in recent years due to the spread of the novel coronavirus across the world. The science journals are striving to provide the best and timeliest research, analysis, and news coverage of the virus. Still, disagreements are rampant across the world. It all comes down to what one knows and the other doesn't. So science is knowledge. In fact, the word *science* is derived from the Latin *scientia,* which means knowledge. Therefore, we can say that science is the pursuit and application of knowledge and understanding. Science has laws and is evidence based. Those who have studied science know that its laws are statements based on repeated experiments or observations that describe a range of natural phenomena.

I said all this about science to say that prayer, in a sense, is a science.

Those who pray must know the laws of prayer for their prayers to be effectual. If we are not aware of the laws of prayer, nothing happens and our prayer life may get quite complicated. The capacity to pray along with knowledge is what we have that is most precious. We may not have a vast knowledge; we may not know a lot about the Bible. But there is at least one thing we can do, and that is to pray.

The Bible teaches that different Christians have different spiritual gifts given to them by the Holy Spirit. As the apostle Paul said to the Corinthians, "There are different kinds of spiritual gifts, but the same Spirit" (1 Corinthians 12:4). Now if you believe you have received the Holy Spirit from God, you have the power to pray. I encourage you to use it for His glory. The knowledge of God's Word is an important factor for effectual prayer for in anyone who claims to be a Christian. Immerse yourself in God's Word. Prayer has the capacity to save you in times of trouble. And as you walk with the Lord, you will have plenty to say about your knowledge of God and the power of prayer.

I wrote this book to help you change your approach toward prayer. It will teach you many things, including wasted time, repetitions, the use of clichés, etc. In this book, you will realize how close God is to you; He is not an old man in a white robe sitting on a recliner trillions of miles away in heaven. This is a book for anyone who wants to understand praying according to God's will.

Chapter 1

Praying according to God's Will

As believers in the Lord Jesus Christ, our highest goal should be to bring glory to Him (1 Corinthians 10:31). This should include praying according to His will. It is crucial that we ask for wisdom as we pray. "If any of you lacks wisdom, he should ask God, who gives generously to all without finding fault, and it will be given to him" (James 1:5). In asking for wisdom, we must also trust that God, in His grace, is willing to answer our prayers. We should not doubt. The scripture is clear about that. "But when he asks, he must believe and not doubt" (James 1:6). I must say that praying according to the will of God includes asking for wisdom to know His will. And as we ask for wisdom, we should understand that is also crucial to ask in faith, for it is by faith that we trust the will of God. When we pray to God, we always hope He will answer our prayers. Yet does God answer all our prayers? If He does, what kind of prayers does He answer? If He doesn't answer all prayers, then why doesn't He?

The prayer that God answers is one that is prayed according to His will. If that is the case, then we must know how to pray according to God's will. First, we must ask for wisdom to trust and accept the will of

God. And in asking for wisdom, we must also trust that He is willing to answer our prayers.

The will of God is a big topic in scripture. We should do our best to understand it. It is extremely important for believers to devote some time trying to understand the will of God and to discern it. Theologically, according to scripture, there are two primary forms of the will of God. There's God's sovereign will, which is the planning of His sovereignty in His own counsel not known to us, and there's His revealed will, which is written on the pages of His Word. The sovereign will of God is a secret that no one can know, but His revealed will can be read in His Word. We will waste our time if we try to discern the sovereign will of God. As believers, the best we can do is to commit our lives to understanding and living inside the boundaries of the revealed will of God in His Word.

In His sovereignty, God desires everything to be done in heaven and on earth according to His sovereign will. When God made humans in His image, He made them to have desires that align in perfect harmony with God's own desires. This is the great privilege of being like God, which means as God feels and wishes, humans can do the same as well; the Bible calls this being in the likeness of God. The likeness of God is a divine gift added to basic human nature, which consists of the moral qualities of God. He created us with these moral qualities. Our image contains the natural attributes of God. However, we lost these natural attributes and the likeness of God when Adam fell. His humanity was spoiled by sin, and he remained in such condition until he became anew in the new Adam, Christ Jesus.

Humans needed this relationship lost in Adam to become whole again. Having a personal relationship with God begins the moment we realize we need Him, admit we are sinners, and in faith receive Jesus Christ, His Son, as our Savior. God always desires to be close to us and have a relationship with us. Adam and Eve knew God intimately and personally before the fall. They walked with Him in the garden and talked directly to Him. That's why they didn't have to pray or fast—because everything they needed was there, most importantly their intimate relationship with God. They could engage in conversations with God without that medium called prayer. Adam and Eve lost that privilege, and as a result, humans began to have needs and began to call on the name of the Lord (Genesis 4:26).

This personal relationship with God is not hard to find. As soon as we have surrendered ourselves to Christ, we receive the Holy Spirit, who begins to work on our hearts. We begin that relationship with God again. Prayer and the reading of the Word of God are the means that keep this relationship healthy. We should pray without ceasing, read the Bible, and join others in fellowship. All these things will help us maintain a solid relationship with God and grow spiritually. Trusting in God and praying to Him each day will help us to get through the days because we believe He is our sustainer. This is the way to have a relationship with Him, and that's what He desires. God's desire is to change our desires to His desires.

The Will of God

The scripture plainly reveals the will of God for us. The will of God are things that, essentially, He considers good for us. His will is revealed in His precepts. These precepts are commands we need to obey and live by. We, as believers, are to live according to God's will revealed in His inspired Word. He reveals His will for our lives in His Word. That's why it is so crucial for us to know what God says in His Word.

Christians routinely violate the will of God. Oftentimes we divide over the nonessentials while neglecting or ignoring the essentials of the faith. Some things may be good but not essentially good for us. Some things are essential to salvation, and some are not. Scripture tells us that our sovereign God has already planned what is best for us, but we have to be mindful of His priorities, and that will help us follow His plan. God's priorities and will for us are revealed in scripture. The Word of God specifically mentions at least seven things that are part of His will for our lives. These are important for us to know as we pray so that we can pray according to God's will. In fact, scripture says, "For this is the will of God, your sanctification ..." (1 Thessalonians 4:3).

Although the Bible speaks of the will of God in several different ways, it is important to understand the differences. There are, however, two clear and different meanings for the term "will of God" in the Bible: God's sovereign will and God's will of command.

God's Sovereign Will

The sovereign will of God simply means God sovereignly controls all that comes to pass. Jesus spoke of the sovereign will of God in Gethsemane when He prayed. He said to His Father, "My Father, if it be possible, let this cup pass from me; nevertheless, not as I will, but as you will" (Matthew 26:39). It was the sovereign will of God that Jesus die. As we read in the book of Acts, "In fact, this has happened here in this very city! For Herod Antipas, Pontius Pilate the governor, the Gentiles, and the people of Israel were all united against Jesus, your holy servant, whom you anointed" (Acts 4:27–28). This was God's plan, His decree. Nothing could change it. God's sovereign will is unalterable. That's what the Bible alludes to when it says, "God is not a man, that He should lie, nor a son of man, that He should repent" (Numbers 23:19). God cannot change His mind. It is important to remind you that although God cannot change His mind, we should never forget He has a good purpose for His people who cannot be hindered (Romans 8:28). However, we are to live our lives according to His will of command.

God's Will of Command

God's will of command is the second meaning of His will in the scriptures. Basically, God's will of command is what He commands us to do. We get in trouble when we violate His will of command. Unlike the sovereign will, believers can disobey and fail to do God's will of command. The sovereign will is God's decree; believers do it whether they believe in it or not. We have no choice in the matter. We have to obey God's will of command. Jesus said, "Not everyone who says to me,

'Lord, Lord,' will enter the kingdom of heaven, but the one who does the will of my Father who is in heaven" (Matthew 7:21). Not all do the will of God. And as a result, many will miss the boat. We must live by the Lord's will of command.

The Bible is to be our guide when it comes to choices we make in life. Namely, it needs to be our guide in our choice of spouse, vocation, where to live, and so forth. Of course, the Bible does not tell us what profession to choose, but it does tell us God has given us certain gifts (1 Corinthians 12; Ephesians 4:1–16). It also tells us to seek out wise counselors (Proverbs 11:14). Likewise, the Bible does not tell you whether you should marry Julie or Julienne, but the book of Proverbs describes the godly woman for any man who is looking for a wife (Proverbs 31:10–31). So you should look for someone who embodies the qualities found in this passage. If a man of God should look for a woman with Proverbs 31 qualities, a single woman should, likewise, look for a man worthy of such a good and godly character. If we make decisions based on God's will of command, we will not go wrong and we will see His plan fulfilled in our lives.

Now when we pray, we must pray as God commands. Prayer is an important part of the Christian life. Because it plays such an important role in our lives, we want to make sure we pray according to God's will so that it can be acceptable to Him. We can't afford not to pray, because prayer for us is like breathing. Martin Luther understood how indispensable prayer is in the life of a Christian when he wrote, "To be a Christian without prayer is no more possible than to be alive without breathing." The moment we stop breathing, we die. Likewise, when we stop praying, we stop communicating with God. This results in a spiritual deficiency. Jesus said, "Men ought always to pray." For our prayer to be effectual, we must pray according to God's will. Our prayer must possess the characteristics of the will of the Lord in order to render it acceptable to Him. Without these characteristics, it may have no effect. The Bible says some prayers are an abomination to God. They are unacceptable to Him.

The Lord invites us to pray, and He takes pleasure in our prayer. By

His spirit, God inspires within our hearts the disposition to pray. Such prayer needs to be addressed according to His will.

God's Perfect or Permissive Will

Paul speaks of the perfect will of God in Romans 12:2. "Don't copy the behavior and customs of this world, but let God transform you into a new person by changing the way you think. Then you will learn to know God's will for you, which is good and pleasing and perfect."

When we turn our backs on the world and let our minds be renewed by God, He then enables us to discern and experience His will for us. God's will is His plan and purpose for us, which is good and pleasing to us and to God.

This plan is complete and has no flaws. It is the perfect will of God for us. God is omniscient. In His omniscience, He knows what He will accomplish in us.

He already knows what we will do before we even thought of doing it. He knows what we would do in any given circumstance. So His plans for us will never fail; they will never be flawed by anything. God's plan and purpose for each and every one of us is for our good and for His glory. The scripture says in Romans 8, "And we know that God causes everything to work together for the good of those who love God and are called according to his purpose for them" (Romans 8:28).

There is also what is called God's permissive will. God's permissive will is what He allows, even though it is sin. We can see in the book of Genesis how God allowed Joseph's brothers to betray him and to deceive their father so that He might bring the Israelites to Egypt, where God would spare them and they would greatly multiply. "You intended to harm me, but God intended it all for good. He brought me to this position so I could save the lives of many people" (Genesis 50:20). In His permissive will, God allows man to reject the gospel, to willfully disobey His precepts, to persecute the Christians, and to do despicable things to them. Yet in all of this, He remains in control, and His purposes are being accomplished. In His sovereign will, He often permits men to violate what gives Him pleasure. So as you can see, God's permissive will is never outside His sovereign will. He allows those things that will lead to the accomplishment of His sovereign will.

Oftentimes as we pursue a new endeavor, we seek God's direction to find out if our plan aligns with God's will; we pray about it. If we're successful, we often say it's God's will for us to do this or that. If we're not successful, we say it probably was not His will. This is what we might call the directive will of God. This is God's personal guidance in our lives. This is in accordance with the wills of God discussed above. There are times when God wants us at a certain place, doing a certain thing at a certain time. God doesn't often provide us with a direct and personal revelation of His will. However, we can see His directive will being revealed in some stories in the Bible. For example,

> Paul and Silas traveled through the area of Phrygia and Galatia because the Holy Spirit had prevented them from preaching the word in the province of Asia at that time; so instead, they went on through Mysia to the seaport of Troas. That night Paul had a vision: A man from Macedonia in northern Greece was standing there, pleading with him, "Come over to Macedonia and help us!" So we decided to leave for Macedonia at once, having concluded that God was calling us to preach the Good News there. (Acts 16:6–10)

This was the directive will of God revealed to them.

We can also see the directive will of God as He gave direct guidance to Philip when "an angel of the Lord said to him, 'Go south down the desert road that runs from Jerusalem to Gaza,'" where Philip met the treasurer of Ethiopia, a eunuch of great authority under the *kandake,* the queen of Ethiopia. God gave him direction to go there and share the gospel of Christ with him. This is the directive will of God.

Furthermore, God's directive will revealed to Peter and Cornelius in Acts 10:1–23. As you can see, God does guide us personally and directly, but it appears this is not as common as we would like to see it. God's directive will seems to be required at certain points of our life when specific guidance is needed to fulfill a task according to God's sovereign will.

God reveals His will to us in His Word. So living according to His revealed will should be the main purpose of our lives. To know the will of God we should live by His Word, immerse ourselves in it, and fill our minds with it. As we pray, the Holy Spirit will transform us through the renewing of our minds so that we may experience what is good, acceptable, and perfect, which is the will of God.

Chapter 2

The Mystery of Prayer

Prayer is a mystery. When we pray, we talk to a person we can't see with our naked eye. But we must believe that He exists. We go to God by faith. Hebrews 11:6 says, "And without faith it is not possible to be well-pleasing to him, for it is necessary for anyone who comes to God to have the belief that God is, and that he is a rewarder of all those who make a serious search for him. In reality, we can't simply say God exits. God is. He is a transcendent being, infinite, self-existing, and without origin. God was, God is, and He will ever be. He is a strong and powerful Person who is at the same time loving, kind, gracious, and merciful. When we approach God through prayer, we experience a supernatural presence of truth and goodness that is flowing through us. His name is God the Father, Son, and Holy Spirit. He is a personal God.

This personal God loves all man. He created man with gifts, abilities, and talents. He created us with responsibility for who we will become, what we will do, and the difference we will make in this world based on these gifts. God made us in Him with purposes to love, bless, and transform this world. As Paul said to Ephesians, "For we are God's handiwork, created in Christ Jesus to do good works, which God prepared in advance for us to do" (Ephesians 2:10). It's a calling with high responsibility. And I believe every call is personal. If you don't do what He designed for you to do, they do not get done. Think about it.

Prayer is a supernatural phenomenon. It is a direct line of communication between us Christians and the Lord. Therefore, when we pray, we must approach as something supernatural, and we should not take it lightly. Prayer is great source of power. But it remains untapped in the world. Through the power of prayer God releases His resources to us. It is a privilege for us to go to the Lord in prayer. He makes it possible because of His great love. We should never disregard this great blessing. Some Christians neglect prayer, and others think prayer is a personal gift imparted on believers by the Holy Spirit. Did know that prayer is not a spiritual gift? As mysterious it is, prayer is not a spiritual gift given to a privileged few. Rather, prayer is an invitation to approach the throne of God. It says in the book of Hebrews, "Let us therefore come boldly unto the throne of grace, that we may obtain mercy, and find grace to help in time of need" (Hebrews 4:16).

Prayer is a precious gift to every believer. We are all called to pray, not simply in the privacy of our own homes but together with other believers. Although time alone with God in prayer is critical to our personal growth, the scriptures tell us that God responds in uniquely powerful ways when believers gather corporately to pray. Corporate prayer is good for the church, but we need our personal time with the Lord. It is essential to our personal growth and communion with God. It says in the book of Acts that the early church joined together constantly in prayer (Acts 1:18). The early church met daily and devoted themselves to the apostles' teaching, the breaking of the bread, to the fellowship, and to the prayers (Acts 2:42). God uses corporate prayer to strengthen the church in the midst of intense persecution (Acts 4:23–31). The church body today may not be facing the same battles the early church faced, but they are nonetheless fierce. If we are concerned about the spiritual, physical, and emotional health of our children and families, we must pray for them. The church of God should emphasize corporate prayer and organize prayer meetings.

Prayer is a mystery because it opens up a new dimension that reaches into the depths and intricacies of the unknown, but a dimension where our Lord lives and moves. As we said before, prayer is a line of communication between us and God. Therefore, it is a two-way communication system whereby the channel is God planning everything, not man. So it is imperative that we understand what our side of this communication involves. Prayer is a mystery.

Chapter 3

What Should We Pray For?

One day Jesus told his disciples a story to show that
they should always pray and never give up.
—Luke 18:1

According to Jesus, all of us Christians should pray at all times. This is a compelling obligation He taught His disciples, which is a duty for all of us who believe in Him. The apostle Paul, in 1 Thessalonians 5:17 wrote, "Pray without ceasing." Evidently, this is a plain command from God. We are to be constantly in communication with God. Not only does God command us to pray, but He also says we ought to pray all the time! Through prayer, we should continually turn our hearts to God and talk to Him about everything we need until our minds are incessantly in touch with Him.

The first way to pray according to God's will is to pray for things that He commands us to pray for. We can pray for a lot of things. However, where God commands prayer, we can pray with confidence that we are praying according to His will. We are to pray for things pertinent to His commands, meaning the things that He commands us to pray for.

When I was a kid, my parents used to have family devotions every morning before they went to work, except when they had to travel out of town. Oftentimes they got up before the sunrise and departed before we even woke up. At such times, one of the older siblings had to take over all the responsibilities of the house including the morning devotional. One morning, my parents were out of town and my oldest sister asked one of our family relatives to pray during our devotion. She prayed for the travelers everywhere, the strangers who are on our doorstep, missionaries, those who travel by air, by sea, and by car, and for all Bible distributors around the world. The kids found that amusing and laughed. First, they thought her prayer was too long. Because we all tried to get ready for school, they thought such a long prayer might cause us to get to school late. Although we all went to the same school, which was less than two minutes from our house, they still had an issue with that prayer. These kids who are now adults with their own families and children still joke about it from time to time.

Second, they couldn't understand why she had to pray for all these people. If you look at that prayer closely, you'll notice she prayed for strangers on her doorstep, but what she truly asked for is God's protection against her enemies. Then she went on and prayed for the missionaries and others who labor in God's work. She prayed according to God's will. A survey of the New Testament will certainly give us a list that can guide us in how to pray according to God's will of command. It can be exhaustive, and we don't have to pray all of them each time we pray. However, we need to periodically pray through this list so we know for certain that when we pray, we do it according to God's will. Regarding praying according to God's will, there are at least seven commands of God that we need to obey if we want our prayers to be effectual.

My goal in this chapter is to list the seven ways and show you how to reap the benefits when you apply them to your prayer life. There are at least seven commands from the Word of God regarding prayer. The first command from our Lord Jesus regarding prayer is we ought to pray for our enemies.

1. Pray for your enemies.

> But I say to you, love your enemies, bless those who
> curse you, do good to those who hate you, and pray
> for those who spitefully use you and persecute you.
> (Matthew 5:44)

When Jesus ministered on earth, many people refused to follow
Him. He was regarded by many as an enemy of the Jews. He was
recognized as an enemy of the state and was sentenced to death by
crucifixion. To affirm their loyalty to the state, the mob chanted, "We
have no king but Caesar."

Today, mistakenly, many Christians have weakened the term
"enemy" to the point that it lost much of its alarming value. Sometimes,
we even associate with someone who pretends to be a friend when, in
reality, we know he is an enemy. Those friends are your undeclared
enemies. Our enemies are known and unknown.

The staff of a former president of the United States used to have
an "enemies list." They wrote down the names of people who they
believed were hostile to the president. The list included politicians,
journalists, academics, and others. You may not be able to make a
list of your enemies, because there are many known and unknown.
The most dangerous ones are the unknown ones. Speaking of the
unknown enemies, Voltaire, the famous French Enlightenment writer
and philosopher of the seventeenth century, contended, "I pray to God
to deliver me from my friends: I will defend myself from my enemies."
Whether our enemies are declared ones or not, they are our enemies.
Some are visible, and some are not. We are fighting an invisible war.
This is the reason why the apostle Paul declared to the Corinthians,

> Put on all of God's armor so that you will be able
> to stand firm against all strategies of the devil. For we
> are not fighting against flesh-and-blood enemies, but
> against evil rulers and authorities of the unseen world,

against mighty powers in this dark world, and against
evil spirits in the heavenly places. (Ephesians 6:12)

In Jesus's day, the Jews in Israel had real enemies. They have fought their enemies since they have existed as a people—from their slavery in Egypt to the Roman Empire when Jesus was crucified. Israel has been in a constant battle with its neighbors. Telling them to love and pray for their enemies, one might say, sounds unrealistic since they are under attack every day. Yet that is exactly what Jesus said to His disciples. When Jesus gave the command to love and pray for our enemies, He knew it would one day require praying for those who hate us, whether they are declared enemies or not. What Jesus is saying is when we think of those people who hate us, we no longer even see them as enemies. They may see us as enemies, which we are in their eyes, but in our eyes, they should be seen as neighbors. So we do have enemies.

I have heard Christians say they have no enemies. If you are a true believer, believe me: you have a lot of enemies. As believers, we find ourselves in a constant battle against our enemies. They persecute us constantly. In fact, Paul said to Timothy, "Yes, and everyone who wants to live a godly life in Christ Jesus will suffer persecution" (2 Timothy 3:12).

We are confronted with persecution, wickedness, false teaching, and temptation every day in our lives and in the church. Human beings are the agents for much of this evil. You find them everywhere. Are they our enemies? I believe they are. A few years ago, I was invited to speak at a conference in Georgia. I realized how the pastor wanted to make the people aware of their constant battle. Every night during the conference, he asked the congregation to repeat Psalm 144:1 seven times aloud. "Praise be to the Lord my Rock, who trains my hands for war, my fingers for battle." We are in a constant battle against our enemies.

Jesus commands us to pray for our enemies. The questions are these: How do we do that? How should we pray for these people who have hurt us and want to hurt our family? It's a difficult task, but the Word of God gives us specific ways to pray for our enemies.

Pray for the Salvation of Our Enemies

First, we need to pray for their salvation. God can do for them what He did for us, and we need to recognize that. We must pray God will provide to them the gift of grace as He did for us. Ephesians 2:8 says, "God saved you by his grace when you believed. And you can't take credit for this; it is a gift from God." Sometimes, we don't pray for them because we want them to receive what they deserve, which is some kind of punishment. We forgot none of us receive what we deserve.

God asked Jonah to go to Nineveh and "announce my judgment against it because I have seen how wicked its people are." Yet Jonah ran away from the Lord and headed for Tarshish. To him, the people of Nineveh should receive what they deserve, which is God's judgment. During the Holocaust, under the command of Adolf Hitler, approximately 6 million Jews were killed by the Nazi regime. Many Christians prayed for Hitler although he and his collaborators committed such horrific crimes against the Jews.

From the late 1950s to the mid-1980s, the Duvaliers ruled the country of Haiti. It has been reported "as many as 30,000 Haitians were killed, many by execution, under the regime of the two Duvaliers," according to the New York-based Human Rights Watch. Many fervent Christians had prayed for them for decades. They considered it a duty. However, many Haitians, especially the families of the victims, would want the Duvaliers to receive what they deserve. Believers and unbelievers alike were terrified by the actions of the regime's special operations unit within the paramilitary force called Tonton Macoutes. The youths, especially the high schoolers, hated the Tonton Macoutes. Many hoped they would get what they deserve, which is a place in hell. I heard the story of a Haitian Christian man who was so angry with the Duvalier regime that he went so far to say, "If I were to go to heaven and found Papa Doc there, I would ask God to send me back to the earth. I would not want to share the same place with this man!" he exclaimed. That would not be fair.

Likewise, consider all the Christians who, during World War II and after, dutifully prayed for the Nazis. How do you think they would have felt if they got to heaven and discovered that Hitler, in moments prior to his death, had truly repented of his sins and was forgiven by God? How do you think the angry families of the victims of the Duvaliers' regimes would have felt if they discovered Papa Doc had repented of his sins and was forgiven by God? Many of them would have felt cheated, as if it were unfair of God to forgive them after they committed such horrific crimes. They would probably complain, as Jonah did when God spared the Ninevites, "I knew that you are a merciful and compassionate God, slow to get angry and filled with unfailing love. You are eager to turn back from destroying people" (Jonah 4:2).

God is not fair. Fairness means you get what you deserve. As Christians, we should be glad God is not fair to us. Otherwise, none of us would have access to His throne of grace. God is not obligated to accept any of us. He accepts us only by His grace. We need to be grateful for being accepted into the kingdom of God. We don't want God to be fair to us because in reality, the principle of fairness is equal pay for equal work. That's fairness. When you go to work, you want to be paid for the hours you put in. If you noticed a problem on your paycheck whereby you are paid for thirty-eight hours for a forty-hour work week, you would go to your boss to claim the unpaid hours. You would probably say to him or her, "It's not fair to pay me for less than I worked for." You would be right because what you deserve is equal pay for equal work. If God was to give us what we deserve, all we would get is a place in hell, because that's what we deserve. God in His mercy doesn't give us what we deserve, but by His grace, He gives us what we don't deserve: a secured place in heaven.

Jesus commands us to pray for our enemies especially those who are engaged in persecution against us. The reason is because He is a gracious and compassionate God who wants them to change their ways and turn to Him. So we ought to love them and pray for their conversion. Even though they persecute us, we should ask God to show them the same grace and mercy He has shown to us.

Pray God Puts a Limit on Their Evil Actions

If God doesn't restrain the actions of the evildoers, the consequences can be devastating for both sides. It is to the benefit of the evildoers as well as ours that God prevents them from doing more evil. Solomon in Proverbs 28 wrote, "Whoever conceals his transgressions will not prosper, but he who confesses and forsakes them will obtain mercy. Blessed is the one who fears the Lord always, but whoever hardens his heart will fall into calamity." Those who harden their hearts and engage in persecution of God's children will pay for their actions. "In his justice He will pay back those who persecute you" (2 Thessalonians 1:6).

Pray for God's Justice on Them

As believers, we are to call on God's justice on our enemies. Divine justice is to be exercised against the hardened, deceitful, and unjust people. When we pray for God's justice, we should remember justice belongs to Him alone, making sure we ask the Lord to deliver His justice in His way at His appropriate time. Since justice belongs to Him, we must be patient and allow Him to work through the means that He has determined. In asking that divine justice be done, we should be careful to guard our motives. Oftentimes we pray for divine justice, but deep down in our hearts we wish them dead. Praying for divine justice on our enemies is not a substitute for our duty to love them. While we must leave vengeance to God, we should never forget what He commands to do. Paul wrote the following to the Romans:

> Dear friends, never take revenge. Leave that to the righteous anger of God. For the Scriptures say, "I will take revenge; I will pay them back, says the Lord. Instead, If your enemies are hungry, feed them. If they are thirsty, give them something to drink. In doing this, you will heap burning coals of shame on their heads."

Don't let evil conquer you but conquer evil by doing good. (Romans 12:19–21)

As we pray for our enemies, we should remember we ourselves were enemies of God. Therefore, we should be grateful that He allows us to appear before His throne of grace to pray for our enemies. We should be thankful for the grace of God and let Him know clearly that we are so thankful that we even want our enemies to receive it too. If they refuse God's grace and harden their hearts against Him, then it will be up to God to exercise His justice on them as He has determined.

2. Pray for God to send missionaries.

The harvest is great, but the workers are few. So pray to the Lord who is in charge of the harvest; ask him to send more workers into his fields. (Luke 10:2)

The second command from the Lord Jesus Christ is to pray for God to send missionaries to His fields. The ministry of the gospel calls men to receive Christ as their Savior. Through His Spirit, the Lord empowers His faithful servants and sends them out to the field. They respond to God's call and embark on a missionary journey to expand the kingdom of Christ. Any journey with the goal to expand or strengthen God's kingdom, short or long, is always a difficult one. The enemy of Christ, the devil, will always stand in the way of His servants to prevent His mission from being accomplished. The devil will hide behind wicked men to do his evil work. Missionaries are often attacked by evildoers and wicked men of this world. As Paul said to the Corinthians, "For we are not fighting against flesh-and-blood enemies, but against evil rulers and authorities of the unseen world, against mighty powers in this dark world, and against evil spirits in the heavenly places" (Ephesians 6:12). Our warfare is with principalities and powers and not with people. Many times, it is through people that these rulers of the darkness of this world reveal their work. Therefore, the missionaries whose primary assignment is to work with people are in great need of prayers from fellow believers.

Specific Prayers for Missionaries

Since God commands us to pray for missionaries, how can we be specific in our prayers? If we do not rely on the Bible for guidance, it can be difficult to know exactly how to pray for missionaries. Scripture gives us several specific ways to intercede effectively for those who bring the gospel to the world.

Pray for the Effectiveness of God's Word

The mission purpose is to communicate the message of the gospel and that it is received by the people to which it is intended to reach. This purpose can be hindered when people are spiritually blinded to what God is trying to teach. We should pray for the missionaries so that they will be able to communicate the message of the gospel clearly in a manner that people can understand.

In order for the message to reach its intended user, the missionaries who minister cross-culturally will need some language and communication skills. Our responsibility is to pray they will be able to communicate well. So they must learn the language and the culture of the people God sends them to work with if they are to be effective. A missionary who doesn't have good language skills will not be able to communicate the Word of God effectively. Understandably, not every missionary who learns a new language will be a great orator in that new language, but we can pray God will give them the skills they need to teach His Word and make a lasting impact on the people.

Pray for Their Protection

Missionaries not only need our prayer for effectiveness as they proclaim God's Word, but they also need our prayer for God's protection. The enemies of Christ are always at war with us. Therefore, they are against the advancement of the gospel of Christ. So as missionaries engage in proclaiming Christ among the unreached people of the world, without a doubt the forces of the devil will attack them. So we must fervently pray for their protection and deliverance from enemies. That's why Paul asked the Thessalonians to pray for his protection so that the devil does not attempt to disrupt his missions. He wrote, "Pray, too, that we will be rescued from wicked and evil people, for not everyone is a believer" (2 Thessalonians 3:2).

Missionaries count on us for prayers. We must pray for their protection against the wiles of the devil. Some governments are antagonistic to missionary work. We are to pray for their protection against such governments. We must pray they have good relationship with the government of the country where they minister. Lastly, pray for protection against sickness, accidents, tragedies, discouragement, and persecution.

Pray for Their Physical and Emotional Needs

Going to a new area to do mission work, perhaps learning a new language and culture can be exciting. However, there are other issues that the missionary may be concerned with. Depending on where God sends someone, life may look like paradise on earth or the North Pole. Either way, the new climate may bring with it disease, allergies, or some physical labor with which the missionary is not familiar. We ought to pray for them so that they don't get frustrated and become depressed. You need to pray for their interpersonal relationships with other missionaries, intrapersonal relationship with themselves as they go through cultural stress, and work anxiety. If a missionary is not emotionally stable, he or she cannot function effectively in the mission field.

Pray for a Good Relationship with God and Their Family

Missionaries must have a good relationship with God and His Word. They need this relationship to teach the Word of God with confidence and authority. As believers, we should pray they would have a desire to study God's Word and teach it with passion and ease. Pray they find encouragement in the Word of God through prayer.

Missionary life is difficult. It can put a strain of the family. Pray missionary couples will cultivate their relationship with one another and with their children. The relationship within the missionary's family is crucial and is a great example to the people to whom they minister. Or Satan can use it to destroy their spiritual progress in the field.

3. Pray to not enter into temptation.

> Keep watch and pray, so that you will not give in to temptation. For the spirit is willing, but the body is weak! (Matthew 26:41)

The third command is to pray to not give in to temptation. The Bible defines temptation as the inclination to commit sin. It is the desire to do something that brings joy or satisfaction momentarily, which may be later regrettable.

Temptation may come through different channels, including relational, social, economic, legal, and psychological. Temptation can also be performed by inducing a person into committing an act by manipulation. Temptation is a dangerous thing we can easily fall into. One day, as Jesus taught His disciples in Judea, they asked Him to teach them how to pray. He said to them, "This is how you should pray, 'Father, may your name be kept holy. May your Kingdom come soon. Give us each day the food we need, and forgive us our sins, as we forgive those who sin against us. And don't let us yield to temptation'" (Luke 11:2–4). Jesus knew how powerful the desires of temptation are, because He was tempted three times without yielding to it. As the letter to the Hebrews says, "For we do not have a high priest who is unable to sympathize with our weaknesses, but one who in every respect has been tempted as we are, yet without sin" (Hebrews 4:15 ESV).

Having been tempted several times, our Lord Jesus, the great Shepherd, experienced firsthand the power of temptation. That is mainly the reason why Paul encouraged believers to pray for the ministers of the gospel.

4. Pray for ministers of the Word.

> Pray for us, too, that God will give us many opportunities to speak about his mysterious plan concerning Christ. That is why I am here in chains (Colossians 4:3)

Most Christians sometimes mistakenly think people who need prayer the most are those who have the most noticeable spiritual weaknesses or other problems that life may bring to them. We often base on what we notice our brothers and sisters are going through to say, "Brother so-and-so needs a lot of prayer." Oftentimes we bypass those to whom God has given the most gifts and graces; we don't think they need our prayer when in fact they are also in great need of prayer. Ministers of the Word of God continually need the prayers of the saints. Those in front lines of the battle proclaiming the truth of the gospel are the objects of the flaming arrows of the devil. Satan is looking for every opportunity to run them over. This is the reality for every pastor and other faithful servants who minister in God's field. Therefore, they constantly need the people of God to be praying for them. The pastors of the local church in particular can't do it alone without the prayers of faithful members of their congregation. They need the prayers of the congregants as much as the congregants need their prayers.

Remember pastors are also sheep; they are Christ's sheep. As sheep themselves, they are susceptible to the same weaknesses that their congregants are susceptible to. Moses's sinful anger led him to strike of the rock when the Lord asked him to speak to it (Numbers 20:7–12). David's selfish desires led him to adultery and murder (2 Samuel 11).

Simon Peter's human weakness and frailty led him to his denial of the Lord (Matthew 26:69–75). All ministers of the gospel are faced with the reality of the weakness of the flesh and the attacks of the prince of the world.

There have been a great number of fallen ministers who have brought disgrace to the church and the name of Christ. Satan has the ministers of the gospel and their families as his targets. Since they are in front lines of the battle, Satan's goal is to bring them down and therefore bring dishonor to the gospel of Christ. Church members should pray their pastor and their pastor's family would not fall under the vicious attacks of the enemy—the temptation of the flesh and the world.

Furthermore, pastors are sometimes under great physical attacks and need to be delivered. When the apostle Paul was imprisoned by the Romans, he encouraged the members of the church in Philippi to pray for his release. He wrote, "For I know that as you pray for me and the Spirit of Jesus Christ helps me, this will lead to my deliverance" (Philippians 1:19). In addition, we learn from the book of Acts that church members constantly prayed for Simon Peter when he was imprisoned by Herod. Luke wrote, "Constant prayer was offered to God for him by the church" (Acts 12:5). After his release, Peter went directly to the home where the disciples were praying for his deliverance.

It is important that we understand how powerful the prayers of the saints are for the ministers of the Word. Prayers of the saints are efficacious and can deliver the man of God from harm. God called the pastor to do the work of an evangelist. If he is living under oppression of any kind, he will not be able to proclaim the Word as he should. The success of the proclamation of the gospel is dependent in part on the prayers of faithful believers. Their prayers are needed so that God opens doors for the minsters as they share the Word of God. The apostle Paul understood when he asked the Colossians to be praying "that God would open to us a door for the word, to speak the mystery of Christ, for which I am also in chains" (Colossians 4:3). Believers are to pray for those who are in government authority so that God can soften their hearts to allow the ministers of the gospel to live their lives peacefully as they proclaim His Word.

5. Pray for government authorities.

> Pray this way for kings and all who are in authority
> so that we can live peaceful and quiet lives marked by
> godliness and dignity. (1 Timothy 2:2)

We are glad that God asks us to pray for our leaders. As Christians, we should consider it a privilege to pray for those God placed in authority. As the evangelist Billy Graham said, "It is a great privilege, as well as our responsibility, to pray for our government leaders." Paul encouraged Timothy to pray for all people. "I urge you, first of all, to pray for all people. Ask God to help them; intercede on their behalf and give thanks for them" (1 Timothy 2:1). We have a responsibility to pray for all people, especially for those who are in authority, because prayers of the saints allow the citizens of the country to live their lives in peace and all godliness and holiness. When we all live in peace, it is easier for us to serve God and lead others to Christ, which is ultimately our mission. God's desire is no one should perish, but for all to come to repentance. We tend to pray for ourselves, our loved ones, and others who ask us to pray for them, but we often neglect to petition for government authorities. We do not pray for our leaders simply because the Lord commands us to. But when you look at it, it makes practical sense to do so. When they make bad decisions, their actions can affect the conditions of our lives, which can greatly impact our families, our churches, our workplaces, and our countries. So when a person in the position of authority obeys the will of God, it makes our life easier. If we want to live peaceful and quiet lives marked by godliness and dignity, we ought to pray for our leaders.

Furthermore, as Christians, we do not pray for our leaders merely for our own benefit. Leadership, when it is taken seriously, is a tiring task. Leadership is difficult. Leading God's flock with conviction and competence, teaching with authority, and preaching God's Word with passion are skills set one needs to learn. It's hard enough to lead people even when you have these skills under your belt. However, it is much harder when you don't. Leaders have no excuse not to know the truth about leadership. In fact, God will judge them more strictly than the rest of the flock because they are supposed to know the truth. The Bible says in the Gospel of James, "Dear brothers and sisters, not many of you should become teachers in the church, for we who teach will be judged more strictly" (James 3:1). Leaders carry a degree of responsibility to their followers. They are often the targets of harsh criticism and people criticize often when there is a crisis. If they don't have the wisdom to lead well, they will fail miserably. We should pray for them because we recognize the greatness of their task and because we are grateful for their willingness to lead. Perhaps you are asking what the procedure is. How should we pray for our leaders?

First, we should pray that God will guide them as they lead. Leaders may sometimes feel lost and need some guidance and wisdom while leading the people. It might seem impossible for them to stay the course while dealing with daily stress, struggles, and challenges. But when we pray for them, God will give them the energies they need to face life the right way without feeling lonely. Leaders may sometime feel lonely, especially when facing hard times. The power of prayer is endless. If one is struggling and looking for guidance and wisdom, prayer can be the answer to their struggles.

Second, we should pray that they are wise and that God grants them the discernment and surround themselves with good and helpful advisors. As the wise Solomon said, "Without wise leadership, a nation falls; there is safety in having many advisers" (Proverbs 11:14).

Third, we know God has placed them in authority. Therefore, we should ask Him to use them as He wills. As Paul said to the Romans, "Everyone must submit to governing authorities. For all authority comes from God, and those in positions of authority have been placed there by God" (Romans 13:1).

Fourth, we should pray for their protection. The enemy will try every opportunity and do all that is in his power to make them fall. If he can't get to them, he'll try their family. If the enemy can distort or destroy a leader's family, he will distort and destroy his or her ability to serve. So when praying for ministry leaders, we can pray for them to have strength in the midst of trials and spiritual warfare and to remain encouraged in their work. We can pray for their families because they sometimes feel people put them under scrutiny and are harshly judged in the court of public opinion. Often ministry leaders and their families suffer a great deal because of their work. God commands us to pray for others so that they can be relieved from suffering.

6. Pray for relief from suffering.

> Are any of you suffering hardships? You should pray. Are any of you happy? You should sing praises. (James 5:13)

It makes the most sense to look to Jesus for our answer. During his suffering in the Garden of Gethsemane, he prayed to his Father, "Yet not my will, but yours be done" (Luke 22:42). He also taught us to pray to our Father in heaven and ask His will to be done. Since so many Bible passages tell us to go to God for strength, we don't need to read between the lines to know part of God's will involves suffering.

> We can rejoice, too, when we run into problems and trials, for we know that they help us develop endurance. And endurance develops strength of character, and character strengthens our confident hope of salvation. And this hope will not lead to disappointment. For we know how dearly God loves us, because he has given us the Holy Spirit to fill our hearts with his love. (Romans 5:3–5)

Believers everywhere are subject to persecution. Satan promised to persecute us, and he will do all he can to destroy us. If you are a follower of Jesus Christ, I'm certain Satan hates you and, like a roaring lion, is looking for every opportunity to destroy you. He will use all kinds of schemes to inflict pain and suffering to the believers in Christ. So our responsibility is to pray for believers who face suffering and persecution, which is the seventh command to praying according to His will.

7. Pray for suffering believers.

> Remember what I told you: "A servant is not greater than his master." If they persecuted me, they will persecute you also. If they obeyed my teaching, they will obey yours also. (John 15:20)

Followers of Jesus Christ will suffer persecution; there is no doubt about that. We often forget the fact that as Christians, suffering is part of our walk with the Lord. As He prepared His disciples for coming persecution, Jesus warned them about what is to come regarding their suffering. He told them, "God blesses you when people mock you and persecute you and lie about you and say all sorts of evil things against you because you are my followers" (Matthew 5:11). He didn't say *if* people mock you, persecute, and lie about you. He said *when* they do. So suffering is something we expect to endure if we are true followers of Christ. In fact, Paul said to Timothy, "Yes, and everyone who wants to live a godly life in Christ Jesus will suffer persecution" (2 Timothy 3:12) and "When we are persecuted, we endure it" (1 Corinthians 4:12).

Millions of believers today endure persecution. Scripture says they are our family: they belong to us, and we belong to them. Therefore, we must pray for those suffering persecution. The questions are these: How then shall we pray for them? How shall we pray for the suffering in our global church family? In the letter to the Hebrews, we read, "Remember those in prison, as if you were there yourself. Remember also those being mistreated, as if you felt their pain in your own bodies" (Hebrews 13:3). So we must be sensitive to the suffering of our fellow believers. We ought to pray for those scattered because of war. The world is fighting several wars. And Christians all over the world are suffering. The wars in the Middle East and the Russia-Ukraine war create a lot of economic instability and turmoil around the world. Not to mention the war on the novel coronavirus that changed the course of things in the world.

We are to pray for suffering believers with compassion and empathy and identify with them in persecution as if we were there with them, enduring the same hardships. In light of spiritual conflict and the "day of evil" as Paul told the Ephesians, we are urged "to pray in the Spirit on all occasions with all kinds of prayers and requests. To that end, keep alert with all perseverance, and always keep on praying for all the saints" (Ephesians 6:18).

God is waiting for our fervent, passionate, intense intercession on behalf of His suffering people. Together, with millions of our global church family, we can intercede on behalf of suffering Christians known or unknown around the world.

Chapter 4

Biblical Models of Prayer

Some years ago, and on many occasions as we studied prayer in our church congregation, we went through the acronym ACTS: adoration, confession, thanksgiving, and supplication. This model can be helpful for structuring our prayers. However, we would be inconsistent in our study if we did not also study the Lord's Prayer. This model that Jesus first gave to His disciples has been used by the churches for centuries. Believers have recited this prayer in public worship and in private intercession. It is appropriate to recite the Lord's Prayer in public worship as many churches have sometimes done as part of their liturgy. However, what many people miss is that the Lord's Prayer is not merely something for us to recite aloud like we sometimes do, but it is a model structure that the Lord gave to His disciples for prayer. In Matthew 6:9, where Jesus introduced the Lord's Prayer, He says, "Pray then like this." First and foremost, the Lord's Prayer is an example of the kind of prayer that honors God, and if we look at it carefully, we will see various elements that show us what we should include in our prayers.

If you move through the Lord's Prayer line by line, you should note several things. First, you will see the privilege of prayer. We can call God "our Father" (Matthew 6:9). This is a promise of a familial, intimate relationship with God. Not everyone is a child of God, but only those who believe in Christ alone for salvation (John 1:11–12) can call God "our Father." We have God as our loving Father only if we are in Christ by faith. Second, the first request of the prayer is for God's name to be hallowed (Matthew 6:9). This speaks to the priorities we should have in prayer. Jesus, above all else, asks for God's name to be sanctified— to be honored as holy on the earth. This means that as believers and children of God, we should want above all else that praying that men and women would know and respect the holiness of the Lord and His sovereign reign.

As the Lord continues to teach the disciples how to pray, He then then prays for God's kingdom to come and for His will to be done on earth as it is in heaven (v. 10). It is important to note that Jesus does not here request for God to become King over creation, because He is sovereign over everything by virtue of His being God as the scripture clearly states. "The Lord reigns, let the earth rejoice; let the many coastlands be glad!" (Psalm 97:1). Instead, Jesus asks that people acknowledge God's reign by bowing to His authority and keeping His commandments. God's kingdom is evident wherever people do His revealed will, and Jesus shows us we should ask for people to become willing servants of the Lord.

After praying for the kingdom, Jesus instructs us to pray for our needs. He says, "Give us this day our daily bread and forgive us our debts" (Matthew 9:11–12). The Lord asks us to pray for our needs and ask God for forgiveness. Lastly, we are to pray that the Lord would preserve us from temptation, that we would be kept from situations in which we feel the attack of the world, the flesh, and the devil (v. 13). As we pray to the Lord, we should prioritize in prayer. We should ask first for the sanctifying of God's name and the extension of His visible kingdom. We should not focus only on our own needs. The Lord's Prayer shows us that we should pray for the extension of God's kingdom above all else. As you pray, dear brethren, take some time to pray that God's name would be honored as holy and that sinners would repent and start doing His will.

Paul prayed for the salvation of Israel (Romans 10:1).

We have ample examples in scripture to follow as models of prayer. The apostle Paul had a burden for the salvation of others. He intensely longed that people might be saved. As a true disciple of Christ, an ambassador of the Lord, a pastor, a preacher, an excellent writer, and a martyr, Paul always sought to save souls for Christ. He dedicated his life to seeking the lost and pointing them to the Lord. He understood Christ alone could save them.

The Jews were religious, but despite their religiosity, they were lost. Despite one's religiosity, one cannot be saved by keeping law, doing good works, or by one's morality; we are not saved by our self-righteousness. This is unacceptable to God. We are saved only when we submit ourselves to Christ's righteousness. The Pharisees trusted in their own righteousness, which could never save them. So Paul longed for them to be saved. Because of his burden for their souls, he went to the Lord in prayer for the salvation of the people of Israel.

David prayed for mercy and forgiveness when he sinned (Psalm 51:1–2).

After Nathan the prophet confronted David about his adultery with Bathsheba, he went to the Lord in prayer for mercy and forgiveness. His prayer is based on God's unfailing love and great compassion. This is His covenant love. David understood that. So he appealed to God's loyal and unfailing love that a father would have for his son. He also appealed to God's deep, intimate, caring love that a mother would have for the child in her womb. Because he had committed such a great sin, David prayed to God for great mercy. His desire is God wipes away his sin from His record book.

The early church prayed for boldness to witness (Acts 4:29).

The early church faced real threats as they continued to proclaim the truth of the gospel of Christ. Peter and John were arrested and put in jail for it. When they were released, they were ordered to be silent, but they made it clear to the authorities that they "cannot help speaking about what they have seen and heard" (4:20). How do you think they were able to sustain such determination? They did it through prayer.

They prayed to the sovereign Lord who gave them strength to continue the advances of His church with boldness.

These prayers were according to the will of God, and similar prayers today can also be addressed according to God's will. As with Paul and the early church, we should always be praying for the salvation of others. For ourselves, we should pray as David prayed, always aware of our sin and bringing it before God before it hinders our relationship with Him and hinders our prayers.

Chapter 5

Praying with the Right Motivation

When you ask, you do not receive, because you ask with wrong
motives, that you may spend what you get on your pleasures.
—James 4:3

As believers, we all know prayer is important. All godly people in the
world can testify to that. I've never met a true servant of God who
doesn't understand the crucial nature of prayer. However, there are
many who pray with selfish motives. I have noticed it firsthand having
been an undershepherd for more than twenty years.

For many of us, it seems our motivation for prayer is results oriented.
We simply pray to get answers. Sometimes, we approach God like we
would go to the supermarket with a grocery list. We ask Him and keep
asking until that list is exhausted. This should not be our prime reason
to pray. We understand Jesus said, "Ask and you shall receive," but
prayer is not about asking and receiving. I think this is a selfish way of
praying. Jesus is our greatest example and I believe we should follow
His model in prayer.

Jesus had unselfish motives in prayer. The main reason in seeking

God's will in prayer is to get our wills aligned with His. Many of us pray to get a sense of comfort beyond the realms of the earth, which is not the real purpose of prayer. Sometimes, we have already made up our minds about something, but we still ask God to do His will. This is nothing but a biased prayer.

We pray to God about His will in some area, knowing that we are already leaning in a certain direction. If we truly want God to answer our prayers, we must ask Him first to help our wills to move to a place where we are willing to do whatever is His will. Once we arrive at that place, He will show us through our mind why one alternative is better than another and that is His will for us. This process may take some time, but He will certainly lead us into the right direction. God's will for us is something to search out before making any major decision. When the Lord Jesus chose His closest followers, He prayed all night seeking God's will about that decision (Luke 6:12–16). Maybe He had preferences for them. He may even have had a list in His mind. He probably had Peter and John on the list, maybe not Andrew, Thomas, or Simon the Zealot. Yet through prayer, Jesus yielded to the will of the Father who made it clear to Him that these men should be on the list. Jesus prayed with no selfish motives. We should do the same.

Selfish motives will not be blessed by God. "And even when you ask, you don't get it because your motives are all wrong—you want only what will give you pleasure" (James 4:3). We should also pray, not so that others may see us as "spiritual" by repeating clichés but mostly in private and in secret so that our Heavenly Father who hears in private will reward us openly. Our Lord Jesus said, "When you pray, don't be like the hypocrites who love to pray publicly on street corners and in the synagogues where everyone can see them. I tell you the truth, that is all the reward they will ever get" (Matthew 6:5–6).

When we search out God's will, we pray so that wills, not our emotions, can be yielded to His will. Whatever the result may be, it's God's will and we should accept it. He has a good plan and purpose for our lives. As the scripture tells us through the voice of the prophet Jeremiah, "For I know the plans I have for you,' says the Lord. 'They are plans for good and not for disaster, to give you a future and a hope'" (Jeremiah 29:1).

So as we spend time with God in prayer with the right motivation, He will guide us to good ideas, thoughts, reasons, and He will reveal His will to us. It might take some time, maybe days, weeks, months, or even years. But if we want to know God's will, we must talk to Him about it.

Chapter 6

Hindrances to Payer

Pray for mercy and forgiveness when we sin.
—Psalm 51:1–2

We must pray in total submission to God. A spirit of bitterness, anger, revenge, or hatred toward others will prevent our hearts from praying in total submission to God. Scripture says in Matthew 5:23–24 not to give offerings to God while there is conflict between us and another Christian. Just as the Lord said about our relationship to other Christians, God does not want the offering of our prayers until we have reconciled with our brothers and sisters in Christ. Such attitude will hinder our prayer. The Bible clearly says there are hindrances to prayer. Sometimes we feel like our prayers are going nowhere. It's like they hit the ceiling of our house and go no farther. The reason being is there are hindrances to prayer. The Bible gives a long list of these hindrances that all of us should be aware of if we want God to give us the desire of our hearts.

First, we need to confess our sin. This is a major hindrance and probably the most common obstacle to our prayers. David said, "If I had not confessed the sin in my heart, the Lord would not have listened" (Psalm 66:18). When we confess our sin, God forgives us and remembers it no more. It says in book of the prophet Isaiah, "I, I am he who blots out your transgressions for my own sake, and I will not remember your sins." This means God doesn't hold us accountable anymore for that sin we committed. And in the first letter of John, scripture says, "But if we confess our sins to Him, He is faithful and just to forgive us our sins and to cleanse us from all wickedness" (1 John 1:9).

Second, we need to forgive those who sin against us. Jesus told the disciples if they want God to forgive their sins, they must forgive those who sin against them. He said, "If you forgive those who sin against you, your Heavenly Father will forgive you. But if you refuse to forgive others, your Father will not forgive your sins" (Matthew 6:14–15). When a person refuses to forgive another, he is hurting himself because his lack of forgiveness will inevitably create bitterness. A person cannot pray with bitterness and expect blessings.

Third, unforgiveness will put stress in our relationships. An unforgiving spirit strains relationships, especially in marriage. First Peter 3:7 says, "You husbands in the same way, live with your wives in an understanding way, and show her honor as a fellow heir of the grace of life, so that your prayers will not be hindered." Jesus said, "Whenever you stand praying, forgive, if you have anything against anyone" (Mark 11:25). If you hold on to resentment or unforgiveness toward anyone or anything, it will be a primary hindrance to your prayer life.

Fourth, failure to spend time in the Word of God will hinder our prayers. Scripture says in the book of Proverbs, "If anyone turns a deaf ear to my instruction, even their prayers are detestable" (Proverbs 28:9). To hear God's voice, we must spend time with Him. If we trust God but do not spend time with Him, we may not hear Him. To hear God, you must give Him undivided attention. That means you cannot let yourself be distracted by other things. You must get alone with God and be quiet. The Bible says, "Be still, and know that I am God" (Psalm 46:10). So as you can see, in order to hear God, we have to get alone with Him, read His Word, and be quiet.

Fifth, our failure to pray in faith can also hinder our prayers. The

Bible says, "You can pray for anything, and if you have faith, you will receive it" (Matthew 21:22). Christians sometimes pray without faith. They pray but do not expect God to answer their prayers because they use prayer as a last resort, not because they believe God will give them what they asked for.

Prayer is an amazing tool God has provided to us for direct access to His throne. It is a great resource we have, and we should use it continually. However, if we misuse this tool, we run the risk of robbing ourselves of the blessings of God.

Chapter 7

Pray with Thanksgiving

We have so much to be thankful for. And our prayers should reflect that. As believers, we all have experienced the grace and peace of God. The peace of God is a state of mind that all of us who have Jesus in our lives possess. It gives our spirit a tranquility that nothing else in this world can. This peace comes from God and is consistent with His character. If you have God in your life, you also have His peace. And the peace of God transcends all circumstances of life.

The grace of God is His favor, blessing He bestows upon all of us. Grace is a continual theme in scripture. The word translated *grace* in the New Testament comes from the Greek word *charis,* which means "favor, blessing, or kindness." We can be kind to others and extend grace to them, but in scripture, when the word *grace* is used in connection with God, it has a more powerful meaning. We are saved by grace, and this is a decision made by God to bless us rather than curse us because of our sins. In reality, that is what we deserve, but He chose to bless us instead. It is His kindness to save the undeserving. That alone is a reason for us to be thankful.

The Christians in the church of Thessalonica experienced great trials. Paul, with a shepherding attitude, exhorts them in his letter to be joyful always, thankful in all circumstances, and pray continually. Paul wrote, "Always be joyful. Never stop praying. Be thankful in all circumstances, for this is God's will for you who belong to Christ Jesus" (1 Thessalonians 5:16–18). Paul commanded the believers there to "never stop praying." This command can be confusing to a lot of Christians today. Obviously, it does not mean we need to keep our head bowed and eyes closed all day long. Paul is not saying we need to talk to God without stopping, but he is asking us to keep an attitude of prayer constantly, which means in our conscience, we must be aware God is with us all the time. Therefore, He engages in our thoughts and actions constantly.

You can always find something to be thankful for, no matter how burdened you are by your wants or needs. Even those who suffer the most in this life have the offer of heaven before them; the blessed hope and the redeeming love of Christ provide a reason to be grateful to God. So do not worry about anything; instead, pray about everything. Tell God what you need and thank Him for all He has done. Pray with thanksgiving.

Chapter 8

Pray with Persistence

Persistence in prayer is for us who pray, not God who asks us to pray. God knows everything and hears us the first time we pray. However, Jesus told His disciples a story to show them that they should always pray and never give up (Luke 18:1). There should never be a time in our lives when we give up and stop praying. God never rejects our prayer if we do not cease to pray. We fail in our prayer when we stop praying. We should persevere in prayer and not quit because we have not received an immediate answer. Part of praying according to God's will is believing, whether His answer is yes, no, or wait. We accept His judgment, submit to His will, and continue to pray. That should be our attitude when we pray because perseverance requires patience and a great deal of waiting.

Jesus told the disciples not to give up because He knows sometimes God delays in answering our requests and when He does, we are disappointed, discouraged, tempted to give up, and lose heart. Wholeheartedly, Jesus wanted to teach them a lesson of faith in prayer, which is why He ended the parable with the question "When the Son of Man comes, will He find faith on the earth?" So when God delays in answering our prayers, He is assessing our faith.

We need to persevere in prayer. If we always receive exactly what we asked the first time we asked, we will begin to treat God as a light switch that turns on the light each time we flip it. God asks us to persist in prayer because persistence compels us to wait on God. Our persistence in prayer deepens our relationships with God and compels our hearts to examine what we want most. Is it God's will we want? Or do we want God even more than what we asked for? If not, then it would be uncharacteristic of God to give us what we ask for even if it is a good thing, because to do it would be out of His own character.

Persistence in prayer requires patience and waiting. It is the foundation of spiritual growth, spiritual vitality, and spiritual health! Sometimes, you will get frustrated by a long wait, but do not let your frustration make you lose heart. Naturally, we are inclined to use God and not to love God, but frustrations in prayer can remove impurities in our hearts and give way for God to give us what our hearts desire.

Often we pray for things. However, when we do not have the answer we expect, we lose heart. This works for our advantage. The reason is God sees our hearts and realizes we have given up. So God temporarily holds the blessings. If we were to get what we want right away, we would depart and no longer pray. Therefore, God protects us from that by making sure that we concern ourselves with Him more closely and devote ourselves to prayer. This is part of His strategic plan to nurture our relationship with Him so that we may depend on Him more than anything we would want in life.

Persistence in prayer is vital to our spiritual growth. God uses it to cleanse our desires, mold us, and even transform those desires, which as a result will change how we pray. When God transforms our desires by our persistence in prayer, our hearts gradually get closer to the heart of God's will. Then He answers our prayers according to His will.

Having a good relationship with God is not a guarantee that He is going to answer all our prayers as asked. Everything is dependent upon His will. You might have been praying for something for yourself or your family for years and it did not happen. You watched things deteriorate right in front of eyes and there is nothing you could do about it. You know your heart is right and your relationship with God is good

43

as it can be. Still, God did not answer your prayers as asked. You say to yourself, "Since I've failed in my prayers, let me change my strategy by asking God to show me why I failed. Perhaps I'll break through." That is not a bad idea. Why does God not answer prayers that sometimes appear in line with His will?

One reason is God wants us to rely on His grace, power, and strength, not on our own. The apostle Paul prayed to God three times to remove something he called a "thorn in the flesh" that he had, which he says was a messenger from Satan to torment him and beat him down. In his prayers, he asked God to remove it, but He did not. Instead, God said, "My grace is all you need. My power works best in weakness" (2 Corinthians 12:9). Paul did not say what that thorn was, but without a doubt, it was a painful thing. When God did not answer his prayer as asked, Paul changed the way he prayed. Now he asked God to help him to rely on His grace, strength, and power, which were made perfect in Paul's weakness.

God requires persistence in prayer. You may have had your share of frustrations in prayer. Let me urge you to persevere in it. Take heart. Perseverance does not guarantee you will get what you asked God for every time you ask, but you will get something better if you persevere. Perseverance in prayer will get you closer to God, which fulfills your heart's deepest desire. You should never think God does not answer your prayers. The answer you get may not be what you wanted or not exactly how you wanted it, but He does give an answer.

God is always pursuing us. He wants us to persist with Him as He has consistently persisted with us. The Bible is the story of God, who is always pursuing a relationship with humankind. In Genesis 3, God asked Adam, "Where are you?" because He pursued Adam. In His pursuit, God wanted to reconstruct that relationship broken by the sin of disobedience. God is still pursuing us today. Therefore, you should never forget this. God never gives up on you, so do not give up in your prayers. Persist in prayer. Do like Jacob did. He wrestled with the Lord. Wrestle with God in prayer because your life depends on it.

Over the years, I have spoken with many people about their spiritual journey. Based on my interactions with them, I know that most Christians are not satisfied with their prayer life. They lack anticipation and faith, and their time with God feels empty. Most likely, many Christians pray so little and so passionlessly. There are obstacles to our prayer life. Those obstacles are hindrances that block vibrant communication between God and us. One of them is impatience. At some point in your life, you have brought your supplication to Jesus vigorously but did not see the desired results. Unfortunately, as humans, we are by nature weak and get tired often. We get weary of asking and listening when all we perceive is silence. We need to remember that God does not act on our cue. In fact, if we could see the big picture as He can, we would gladly wait for His way and time. But we cannot. It is actually a good thing that we do not receive all that we request. Understanding this concept is a sign of spiritual maturity. When we are completely satisfied with the Lord's presence, our relationship with Him will flourish, even when we do not get all we ask. Then we will grasp what prayer really is. It is not a long want list, but a relationship. Barriers can develop if we persistently cry out to God but nothing changes. We should continue to pray and never cease. Beyond this barrier, we will certainly sense God's presence, where there are peace, joy, and formidable glimpses of His glory. This will be completely satisfying, even if God never gives us exactly what we requested.

Chapter 9

Pray with Total Reliance on God

We do not know what we ought to pray for.
—Romans 8:26–27

The Holy Spirit Prays for Us

Sometimes we are depressed and feel we cannot pray. Know the Holy Spirit prays for us.

Christians believe there is one, and only one, true God, and there are three divine persons in the one God: God the Father, God the Son (Jesus Christ), and God the Holy Spirit. This is called the doctrine of the Trinity. We believe God is real and absolute. He was there before anything else, and He did not come into being but always was. Therefore, nobody made Him the way He is. God simply is. God is His name. When God sent Moses to the sons of Israel, he said, "If they ask me, 'What is His name? What should I tell them?' He said to Moses, 'I am who I am'" (Exodus 3:14). This is the God we rely on when we pray. He is the One who shapes our lives according to His reality, His will.

We must submit to the way God is when we pray. He does not submit to the way we are. That is why He answers prayers according to His will.

The focus of this chapter is to show the Spirit is not some force or power of God the Father as some believe, but He is a person who understands what we go through works along with the Father to help us in our weakness. The Spirit prays for us because we do not know what to pray for as we should. "But the Holy Spirit prays for us with groanings that cannot be expressed in words. And the Father who knows all hearts knows what the Spirit is saying, for the Spirit pleads for us believers in harmony with God's own will" (Romans 8:26–28).

When Paul was in prison in Rome, he was unsure what to pray for. He didn't know whether he should pray for life, ministry, or death. He said to the Philippians, "But if I live, I can do more fruitful work for Christ. So I really don't know which is better. I am torn between two desires: I long to go and be with Christ, which would be far better for me. But for your sakes, it is better that I continue to live" (Philippians 1:22–24). This is a painful situation. Paul relied on the Spirit of God in prayer. It is painful for many Christians who suffer persecutions today. It will become increasingly painful as the price of being a Christian and missionary increases around the world. There are many Christians who are in danger somewhere in the world and wonder, "How should we pray? Should we pray for a safe escape? Or should we resolve to stay and pray for protection? Or should we stay and pray for courage to suffer and even die?" This has been the situation for many Christians in most of the Middle Eastern countries for years.

In a study published by Breitbart News Network in 2015, the author reports, according to the World Watch List (WWL), there are fifty countries where persecution of Christians for religious reasons is most severe. Open Doors USA, a human rights organization that has monitored Christian persecution worldwide since the 1970s, published a disturbing list of countries where Christians suffer persecutions the most. The 2015 report found "Islamic extremism is by far the most significant persecution engine" of Christians in the world today and "forty of the fifty countries on the World Watch List are affected by this kind of persecution."

The World Watch List states in the world today, each month, on average, 322 Christians are killed for their faith, 214 Christian churches and properties are destroyed, and 772 acts of violence occur against Christians.

The ten worst countries for Christian persecution are, in descending order, North Korea, Somalia, Iraq, Syria, Afghanistan, Sudan, Iran, Pakistan, Eritrea, and Nigeria. Of these ten, only North Korea is less than 50 percent Muslim, and only North Korea had a primary "persecution engine" that wasn't "Islamic extremism." It was atheistic communism. The report found the Middle East is still one of the most violent areas of the world for Christians, particularly in areas afflicted by aggression from the Islamic State. More than 70 percent of Christians have fled Iraq since 2003, and more than 700,000 Christians have left Syria since the civil war began in 2011.

Persecution is a way of life for the Christians, but who can bear extreme persecution? In the Sermon on the Mount, Jesus taught His disciples how they will be persecuted because of Him. He told them, "God blesses you when people mock you and persecute you and lie about you and say all sorts of evil things against you because you are my followers" (Matthew 5:11). He told them to "rejoice and be glad, because great is your reward in heaven, for in the same way they persecuted the prophets who were before you." He warned them that they will be persecuted because they are not of the world but have been chosen out of the world, and therefore the world hates them just as it has hated Christ. The Lord exhorted His followers to first count the cost, because there is a price to pay and anyone who is unprepared or unwilling to bear a cross and follow Him simply cannot be His disciple. You see, when you are a disciple of Christ, persecution is inevitable, but just because persecution is inevitable does not mean it is acceptable. Persecution is from the devil and is wicked. It involves oppression, cruelty, betrayal, violence, and injustice. All these things are contrary to God's love.

Now why did the Lord call blessed are those who are persecuted? First, those who are persecuted for Christ are victims. Avoiding persecution is easy. All we have to do is deny Christ. Those who consent to suffer persecution rather than avoid it are those who choose faithfulness over temporal self-preservation, because of their love and faith in Christ. Thus, such believers prove their faith in their Savior. Those who are persecuted for Christ's sake are blessed because of their faith in Him. Through persecution our faith is tested, refined, and proven. In the midst of persecution, the Holy Spirit is our comforter.

The Holy Spirit Is Our Comforter

We must rely on the Holy Spirit in prayer because He presents our prayers to God according to His perfect will and timing. Sometimes, we are in such a hurry that we want things immediately. Some of us even think sometimes the Lord takes too long to give us what we want. We cannot wait so we take matters into our own hands. Many Christians take the Lord's name in vain by saying things the Lord did not say. They say, "God told me," misusing the work of the Spirit. Unfortunately, many so-called ministers of the gospel claimed to have heard the voice of God telling them to do things. But it could be their own thoughts they call God's. It is rare that one hears the audible voice of God. Most of us would say we have never heard the audible voice of God. At best we might have a strong voice or thoughts in our head that we imagine come from God or our own thoughts. I have had conversations with ministers who told me that God told them to take actions in pursuing an endeavor, a dream, or a desire they have nourished for a long time. In the Christian circles, people can take the name of God in vain. It is unbelievable how people make up things and scenarios in the name of God. "The Spirit told me," they often say.

In 2012, a woman of South Carolina who allegedly stabbed her husband said she did it after Jesus told her to kill him "because he is Satan's spawn!" The woman told the police she "was sent to save the world." This woman may have suffered from psychological issues, but this has become a habit for many in the church today. It is one of the hardest habits to break. You often hear some say, "God told me this" or "Here is what the Lord showed me." These are, in many instances, false claims perpetrated by some Christians in the churches today. It's a clear violation of the Word of God. "You must not misuse the name of the Lord your God. The Lord will not let you go unpunished if you misuse his name" (Exodus 20:7).

How do we misuse God's name? Most often in our conversations we mention God's name to elevate our credibility. We want people to believe us so we mention it to add weight to our statement. It is an intentional misuse of His name. When we say, "God told me this," it's not God's name we are thinking of; it is our name's recognition and reputation that we are thinking of. God is the ultimate authority and using His name gives us authority and respectability. So when we misuse God's name, we are trying to uphold our own glory instead of upholding His glory.

What is at issue here is that often we let our emotions lead us rather than the Holy Spirit. When we are controlled by our emotions—by how we feel—we are settling for so much less than what God has planned for us. From a human standpoint, we begin to look at things based on their value, and we do that by the nature of our response to them. One of the greatest problems we face when we are led by our emotions: how we feel is that we are often deceived. Feelings cannot be trusted! Our emotions will deceive us because they often change. Christians who deliberately walk into situations applying the "how I feel about it" method rather than God's truth often suffer dire consequences! If we were to apply the Word of God only when it agrees with our feelings, we would not be walking according to the Spirit as God intends for us.

Thus, we need to rely on the Holy Spirit in prayer. We have the Spirit's help in praying. At the times of our deepest depression or sorrow, the Spirit who understands what we go through works along with God the Father to help us in our weaknesses. When we seek to walk in the Spirit and not in the flesh, we have assurance the Holy Spirit will accomplish His work in presenting our prayers to the Father according to God's perfect will and timing. We are confident He is working all things together for our good (Romans 8:28).

The Holy Spirit is our Comforter. His desire is to comfort us in times of trial, anxiety, and depression. The Holy Spirit comes to us as we pray. We need to seek Him with all our heart. He is there even when no one else appears to care. He is there to comfort us. So let us remind ourselves to comfort one another after we have received comfort from the Lord, who is the God of all comfort. Paul wrote to the Corinthians, "God is our merciful Father and the source of all comfort who comforts us in all our troubles, so that we can comfort those in any trouble with the comfort we ourselves receive from God" (2 Corinthians 1:3–4).

God comforts His children. He is the "God of all comfort," and we can know His peace even in the midst of trials. As Paul wrote to Ephesians, "Praise be to the God and Father of our Lord Jesus Christ, the Father of compassion and the God of all comfort, who comforts us in all our troubles, so that we can comfort those in any trouble with the comfort we ourselves receive from God. For just as we share abundantly in the sufferings of Christ, so also our comfort abounds through Christ" (2 Corinthians 1:3–5). God comforts us in many ways: through the wonderful promises of His Word, through fellow believers, and of course through the Holy Spirit's indwelling. The Spirit is our Comforter, Counselor, Encourager, and Helper. He is always present to bring comfort to the children of God (Psalm 34:18; 139:7–8).

Chapter 10

Pray Systematically

What is systematic prayer?

As you can see, in the word *systematic* is the word *system* with which you are familiar. A system is a plan or method used to put things together for something to work. It is a set of procedures or principles according to which something is done. A system may not work if the procedures put in place are not properly followed. As you know, praying is talking with God. It's a means of communication given to us by God Himself to strengthen our relationship with Him, which is personal. We have been given the privilege to know God personally. He has given us a personal invitation to have His Spirit to live inside us when we believe in Jesus. Through His Spirit, God reveals His nature to us. That's what it means to have a personal relationship with God. We don't just know about God; we know Him personally.

Now why do we need to pray systematically? In the process of communication, there is something called "the sending and receiving of information" that needs to be functional for the system to work properly. If a line is broken or something within the communication system is faulty, it will not work. The systematic prayer is following God's system of communication.

The more effort we put into knowing God's ways through His

Word and His Holy Spirit, the more we will adapt to His will in prayer. The more we adapt to the will of God, the more we will see our prayers answered because the prayers God answers are prayers addressed according to His will.

Oftentimes in our prayers, we tell God what we want to happen. No, it's not done that way, my friend. Prayer is knowing what God desires to happen and aligning our will with that. Praying systematically is staying faithful in prayer for persecuted believers on a regular basis. We are urged to pray in the Spirit on all occasions with all kinds of prayers and requests. With this in mind, be alert and always pray for all the saints (Ephesians 6:18). Praying systematically is praying specifically for things pertaining to God's will, not vaguely. For example, you may have a daily prayer calendar with a systematic listing of nations and persecuted peoples around the world to pray for: the sick people, family of the dying, missionaries, pastors, and so forth.

Chapter 11

Why Does God Want Believers to Pray?

Why does God want us to pray? This is a question that I have been asked on several occasions, often in Bible studies. God wants us to come to Him in prayer and ask for the things we need. Wait a minute. Doesn't God know what we need? After all, Jesus said when you pray, don't babble on and on as people of other religions do. They think their prayers are answered merely by repeating their words again and again. Don't be like them, for your Father knows exactly what you need even before you ask him! So since God already knows what we need, why do we have to go to Him in prayer? Why doesn't He give us the things we want and need and so we would not need to ask? There is a reason God wants us to ask Him before He gives us what He knows we need.

God created Adam and Eve; He did so to have fellowship with man, but when Adam and Eve sinned against Him, that fellowship ended. To resume that fellowship that is so dear to Him, He offered Himself as the holy and sinless sacrifice. God's fellowship with man was resumed through the sacrifice of His only Son, Jesus Christ. Not all men, however, have this fellowship with Him. Only those who have accepted His Son as their Savior, are born again, and are washed in the blood of the Lamb have this great privilege. As believers in Christ, God's manner of fellowship with us is to allow Himself, by the Holy Spirit, to dwell within us and to talk with us through prayer.

So the chief reason God wants us to come to Him in prayer is to have fellowship with us. There are a lot of things that are indispensable for our survival. We do not need to ask God for them because He knows they are must-haves for us. For example, the air we breathe, the water we drink, and the sunlight. These things He gives us freely and without our asking because we cannot live without them. Just like Jesus Himself said, "So if you sinful people know how to give good gifts to your children, how much more will your heavenly Father give the Holy Spirit to those who ask Him" (Luke 11:13). God waits till we come to Him in prayer to give us some things, only because He wants us to spend time with Him.

Furthermore, God wants us to pray because prayer expresses our trust in Him. Our dependence is on God because we are His children. We all know that children from birth rely on parents to provide them with the care they need to be happy and healthy and to grow and develop well. The same is true for us children of the Almighty God. Since our new birth, we depend on God to sustain us through our spiritual journey. God offers His children love, acceptance, appreciation, encouragement, and guidance through His Spirit.

God provides security to His children so that they feel safe to survive in this troubled world. We know we are secure in Jesus. When we come to know Christ as our Savior, we are brought into a relationship with God that guarantees our eternal security. Scripture says in Jude 24, "To Him who is able to keep you from falling and to present you before His glorious presence without fault and with great joy." It is the power of God that keeps us from falling. It is up to Him, not us, to present us before His glorious presence. Our eternal security is a result of God keeping us, not us maintaining our own salvation. So as we pray, we need to be confident in our relationship with our loving Father who provides us with love, protection, and security.

The Lord Jesus Christ said, "I give them eternal life, and they shall never perish; no one can snatch them out of my hand. My Father, who has given them to me, is greater than all, no one can snatch them out of my Father's hand" (John 10:28–29). Both Jesus and the Father have us firmly clenched in their hand. Therefore, no one can separate us from the grip of both the Father and our Lord Jesus. So approach God with that certainty as you pray. God is your Father and cares for you, protects you, and is willing to provide for you.

God expects us to look to Him in prayer. "You can pray for anything, Jesus said, and if you have faith, you will receive it" (Matthew 21:22). Prayer brings us into deeper fellowship with God, and He loves us and delights in our fellowship with Him.

The Effectual Prayer

We all want our prayers to be effective. We pray because we want results. We want prayers that avail much. The key to an effectual prayer is finding out God's will in the matter and pray in agreement with His will. Sometimes we have already decided our will in a matter and we are trying to get God into agreement with us. Or we assume what God would want to do in a certain situation and we say this is God's will for us to do this or that. The scripture says, "And this is the confidence that we have toward Him, that if we ask anything according to His will, He hears us" (1 John 5:14 ESV).

James tells us, "Confess your sins to each other and pray for each other so that you may be healed. The earnest prayer of a righteous person has great power and produces wonderful results" (James 5:16). To find God's will is not always easy. I must say to you in all honesty there will be times when even after you have prayed earnestly, you will not know exactly what God's will is regarding an issue. That has been my experience in prayer. In His sovereignty, He simply will not reveal it to you. When this is the case, you can pray in agreement with what you know about His character as revealed in His Word. You can pray by basing on the principles He established in His Word. An effectual prayer is one that produces results. It can change the acts of God. Failure to ask deprives us of what God would otherwise have given to us. "You want what you don't have, so you scheme and kill to get it. You are jealous of what others have, but you can't get it, so you fight and wage war to take it away from them. Yet you don't have what you want because you don't ask God for it" (James 4:2). God declared He would destroy Israel for their sin. Moses prayed God would spare Israel and He did. God said,

> I have seen how stubborn and rebellious these people are. Now leave me alone so my fierce anger can blaze against them, and I will destroy them. Then I will make you, Moses, into a great nation. But Moses tried to pacify the Lord his God. "O Lord!" he said. "Why are you so angry with your own people whom you brought from the land of Egypt with such great power and such a strong hand? Why let the Egyptians say, 'Their God rescued them with the evil intention of slaughtering them in the mountains and wiping them from the face of the earth'? Turn away from your fierce anger. Change your mind about this terrible disaster you have threatened against your people! Remember your servants Abraham, Isaac, and Jacob. You bound yourself with an oath to them, saying, 'I will make your descendants as numerous as the stars of heaven. And I will give them all of this land that I have promised to your descendants, and they will possess it forever.'" So the Lord changed his mind about the terrible disaster he had threatened to bring on his people. (Exodus 32:9–14)

Effectual prayers change the acts of God. An effectual prayer produces results. It may not be the result you want, or you would hope to get, but it will be a result based on the will of God in the matter. James, our Lord's brother, encourages his readers to pray because prayer is effective, which means God hears His people acts on their behalf. James asked, "Is anyone among you suffering? Let him pray. Is anyone cheerful? Let him sing praise." James's whole point is that prayer is effective. "The effective prayer of a righteous person has great power. Elijah was a man with a nature like ours, and he prayed fervently that it might not rain, and for three years and six months it did not rain on the earth. Then he prayed again, and heaven gave rain, and the earth bore its fruit" (James 5:13–18).

In reference to the prophet Elijah, James says that he was a man with a nature like ours. He was just a man. He was like us. He had a nature like ours. And being just a man like us, he prayed fervently, and God heard. The point is that Elijah was like us, and his prayers were answered; therefore, we should pray, and God will answer our prayer. Our prayer can be effective. And the focus of any effective prayer should be on God, not us. Remember the prayer that God answers is one that is addressed according to His will. Prayer has less to do with the specifics of how we say when we pray and more to do with the One to whom we are praying.

Praying in Jesus's Name

Many of us close our prayers with this phrase: "in Jesus's name we pray. Amen." Others close their prayers with "in Your name we pray. Amen." What does it mean to pray in Jesus's name? First, let me say it's completely biblical to pray in the name of Jesus. Jesus Himself tells His disciples to pray to the Father in His name. There are numerous examples in the gospel of John. At least six times Jesus told His disciples to pray in His name. Praying in Jesus's name is a divine privilege. The Lord says, "You can ask for anything in my name, and I will do it, so that the Son can bring glory to the Father. Yes, ask me for anything in my name, and I will do it!" (John 14:13–14).

As you can see, praying in the name of the Lord is extremely important. He would not have told the disciples to pray in His name if it was not important. The importance of God's name and acting in someone else's name are two important concepts in scripture. A person's name in the Bible represents the essence of the person. It represents the person's personality, character, reputation, and authority. All of these are wrapped up in the name. King Solomon, the wisest man who ever lived, said, "A good name is to be more desired than great wealth, favor is better than silver and gold" (Proverbs 22:1 NASB). There is an immense value in a good name. Your character, your personality, and your reputation are embedded in your name. Besides a man's soul, his name is the most important possession he has. We should cherish our good name because it refers to virtue and integrity. It must be nurtured and respected as a most precious possession.

God's name is highly exalted in scripture. His name declares the greatness of His person. King David says, "O Lord, our Lord, your majestic name fills the earth! Your glory is higher than the heavens" (Psalm 8:1). Jesus taught His disciples to pray by saying, "This, then, is how you should pray: 'Our Father in heaven, hallowed be your name'" (Matthew 6:9 NIV). The name of God is holy. Because we are sinful and God is holy, we have no right on our own to enter His presence. We need a mediator to come between us and God to bring us into God's presence. The Bible teaches Jesus is the mediator between God and man. "There is only one God and one Mediator who can reconcile God and humanity—the man Christ Jesus" (1 Timothy 2:5).

Furthermore, to come in the name of Jesus means that God has authorized us to come on His authority, not on our own. The apostles worked with the authority of Jesus, not of their own authority. They were able to do many sign miracles in His name. The first one was when the apostle Peter, in the name of Jesus, healed the lame man. Peter said, "I don't have any silver or gold for you. But I'll give you what I have. In the name of Jesus Christ, the Nazarene, get up and walk!" (Acts 3:6). Also, Paul rebukes an unclean spirit in the name of Jesus when he said to the demon-possessed slave girl, a fortune-teller who earned a lot of money for her masters, "'I command you in the name of Jesus Christ to come out of her.' And instantly it left her" (Acts 16:18).

Praying in Jesus's name means we are coming before God because of what Jesus did for us. Our prayer is addressed to God our Father through the Lord Jesus. However, this does not mean we cannot pray to Jesus Himself. There are numerous places in scripture where prayers are addressed directly to Jesus Christ Himself. The first was in the choice of a new apostle to replace Judas, who had abandoned the ministry. They prayed to Jesus directly to designate one who alongside them would continue the apostolic ministry. Also, during the early days of the persecution of the church, Stephen appeared before the Sanhedrin after being falsely accused of blasphemes against Moses and God. Because they could not find any fault in him, they persuaded some men to lie about him, saying, "We heard him blaspheme Moses, and even God" (Acts 6:11). Stephen prayed to Jesus directly as they stoned him as he called out, "Lord Jesus, receive my spirit" (Acts 7:59).

In addition, you may be asking whether you can pray directly to the Holy Spirit as we pray to Jesus. The New Testament has no record where prayers are addressed directly to the Holy Spirit, but there is also nothing that forbids such a prayer. Scripture teaches the Holy Spirit is fully God. He relates to us in a personal way and worthy of prayer. Jesus said, "And I will ask the Father, and he will give you another advocate to help you and be with you forever" (John 14:16 NIV). The role of the Holy Spirit in our prayers is to help us and make them effective. So as we pray, we ought to consciously be aware of the presence of God surrounding and sanctifying us through the Holy Spirit. As Paul said to the Ephesians, "Pray in the Spirit at all times and on every occasion. Stay alert and be persistent in your prayers for all believers everywhere" (Ephesians 6:18).

Praying with Faith and Obedience

By now you should realize prayer is based on trust and a personal relationship with God. Therefore, if that trust is broken, the relationship is impeded. God's Word tells us to exercise faith when we pray. Jesus says, "You can pray for anything, and if you have faith, you will receive it" (Matthew 21:22). We read in the book of James, "But when you ask him, be sure that your faith is in God alone. Do not waver, for a person with divided loyalty is as unsettled as a wave of the sea that is blown and tossed by the wind" (James 1:6). Prayer is not wishful thinking. It is a relationship with God as a person. So disobedience to Him will certainly be a hindrance to prayer.

God will not hear the prayers of those who reject his laws. David says, "If I had not confessed the sin in my heart, the Lord would not have listened" (Psalm 66:18). Our obedience to Him is never perfect in this life. Therefore, we need to continually confess our sins to God to obtain access to His throne of grace. We can pray twenty-four/seven, and that will not cut it. Confession of sin to God in prayer is necessary for us to be forgiven so that He can restore us to Himself. Jesus, in the Lord's Prayer, said, "And forgive us our sins, as we have forgiven those who sin against us" (Matthew 6:12). Scripture says in the epistle of John, "But if we confess our sins to him, he is faithful and just to forgive us our sins and to cleanse us from all wickedness" (1 John 1:9). And in James, it says that we should "Confess our sins to each other and pray for each other so that we may be healed. The earnest prayer of a righteous person has great power and produces wonderful results" (James 5:16).

Praying with Humility

Humility is an attitude we should all have when we go to the Lord in prayer if we want to obtain His favor. James says in his epistle, "God opposes the proud, but gives grace to the humble" (James 4:6). Cultivating a humble heart in our prayer life is a challenging task. The reason is we want to be important. We don't usually want to be second or third in a setting because for some of us, it's too humbling to be in a second or third position. We want to be first.

What is humility anyway? Humility is a feeling of lowliness realizing our unworthiness of any favor of God. To be humble is to be modest, lowly, with a disposition to constantly seek God's favor. The humble person keeps himself from the public gaze. Humility does not seek publicity or hunt for high places, and the person who is truly humble does not care for prominence. Humble Christians never exalt themselves.

According to our Lord Jesus, there is a proper and an improper way to pray. He illustrates that in Luke 18 in the parable about the boastful Pharisee and the humble tax collector. The Lord says,

> Two men went to the Temple to pray. One was a Pharisee, and the other was a despised tax collector. The Pharisee stood by himself and prayed this prayer: "I thank you, God, that I am not a sinner like everyone else. For I don't cheat, I don't sin, and I don't commit adultery. I'm certainly not like that tax collector! I fast twice a week, and I give you a tenth of my income." I tell you, this sinner, not the Pharisee, returned home justified before God. For those who exalt themselves will be humbled, and those who humble themselves will be exalted. (Luke 18:10–14)

Jesus tells us not to pray like the hypocrites who pray in public places so others see them. "When you pray, don't be like the hypocrites who love to pray publicly on street corners and in the synagogues where everyone can see them. I tell you the truth, that is all the reward they will ever get" (Matthew 6:5). Some years ago, a member of our church who wanted to justify himself before others and show them how good of a Christian he is stood in front of the whole church assembly and said, "Every Saturday I come here in front of the altar to pray." Maybe this person did come to pray at the church every Saturday, but did he have to publicize that?

According to Henry Blackaby,

> There are two ways to attain high esteem. One is the world's method: Take every opportunity to promote yourself before others, seize occasions for recognition and manipulate your way into the center of attention. The other way is God's way: Humble yourself. Rather

than striving for recognition and influential positions, seek to put others first. Cultivate humility, for it does not come naturally. One of the many paradoxes of the Christian life is that when God sees your genuine humility, He exalts you.

The Pharisee, because of his self-centeredness, exalted and praised himself. Jesus said he went away unjustified, condemned, and rejected by God.

The tax collector, on the other hand, who saw no good in himself, did not take credit for anything good in himself. He cried out, "God, be merciful to me, a sinner." Jesus said he went to his house justified.

Chapter 12

Myths about Prayer

You can't complain to God.

You may be aware of this American saying "You can't complain because no one would listen." Quite often you might have heard someone say, "Stop complaining. You are becoming annoying, and I can't stand it."

What does it mean to complain anyway? According to certain universally excepted definitions, complaining is expressing grief, pain, or discontent about something. People complain about a lot of things, including unhappiness, sickness, discomfort, etc. They complain to express grief, pain, or discontent. Complaining is expressing dissatisfaction or annoyance about something. So people do complain sometimes and for the right reasons. As emotional beings, we complain to express our emotional pain, grief, and discontent. We complain to authorities, our bosses, and our peers. People complain with the hope to be heard and therefore force a course of action that would ultimately change things in their favor. If we can complain to our superior, bosses, and peers to express our dissatisfaction, why can't we complain to God? I believe we can.

In Psalm 142, David says, "I cry out to the Lord; I plead for the Lord's mercy. I pour out my complaints before him and tell him all my troubles" (vv. 1–2). Today, we live in a world full of trouble. It is almost impossible to live in this world without experiencing trouble. Sometimes we have a lot of troubles. If we did not have Christ, these troubles would cripple our lives. We are troubled emotionally, physically, and spiritually. We are troubled within and without. Some troubles we go through are simple and small, and some are big and traumatic. They come in many sizes. The novel coronavirus caused troubles around the world. Everyone is affected by this disease directly or indirectly. The pandemic caused many people to lose hope. As you know, hope is essential to life. Without it, one may descend into deep depression, commit suicide, or simply lie down in isolation and die.

The pandemic creates terror around the world. Many people are losing hope for the future. Truly, hope is essential to life. Since our hope is in the Lord, we see life differently. You have heard the story of an American thirteen-year-old boy named Matthew Stepanek who became famous for his poetry and writings about hope and peace. He suffered from a rare and fatal form of muscular dystrophy called dysautonomic mitochondrial myopathy. Despite all this, Matthew Stepanek inspired many Americans with his hopes and dreams, even though he knew that he may die before his dreams come true. His three older siblings died from the same illness. The condition was unknown until his mother was diagnosed with mitochondrial disease in 1992, after all four of the children had been born. Knowing all this, the boy still had hope.

As a Boston oncologist and author, Dr. Jerome Groopman, wrote in his book *The Anatomy of Hope,* "To have hope under extreme circumstances is an act of defiance that permits a person to live life on his or her own terms." Finding hope in such a time as this can be unnerving for many people. People feel despair and live in increasing fears—fear of economic collapse, fear of sickness, and of course, fear of life and death. Everywhere people are looking for hope, and that includes you. The feeling of fear and anxiety in this time of uncertainty is normal. But you can find hope. Our hope is in the Almighty God who gives assurance in His promises in scripture that we can find lasting hope amid a world that can feel hopeless. Remember what He said in Jeremiah 29:11. "For I know the plans I have for you, declares the Lord, plans for welfare and not for evil, to give you a future and a hope." Hope in the Lord is a realistic expectation of something good you wait for in the future that gives joy and glory based upon the Word of God. The more we long for the future, the less we will dwell on the past. Hope deletes regrets and underlines expectation. It diminishes drag and increases momentum.

During the Holocaust, Viktor Frankl, a Jewish prisoner in one of the Nazi camps who later became a famous neurologist and psychiatrist, made a painful observation during his time in the camp. He observed that every year as Christmas approached, many people in the camps would have great hope because some prisoners would be released on Christmas Day. This hope, one might say, was an irrational hope, but it was hope. Then when Christmas would come and go without a release, hundreds of prisoners would just lie down and die. Without hope, they could not live. Frankl concluded, "It is a peculiarity of man that he can only live by looking to the future."

Life is unpredictable and all of us are faced with challenges and problems. Oftentimes we question our past and wonder what would have happened if things had turned out differently. These thoughts can be consuming and keep us from moving forward in life. Dwelling in the past can lead to anxiety and depression. Let me give you three ways to deal with your past so you do not drag your hope.

First, express your hurt because there are many sources of pain in life. You may have made a mistake, regretted a decision, failed to take an opportunity, hurt someone, or been hurt by someone. Instead of reliving your past over and over in your head, get it out. Tell God, and tell someone you trust. Second, accept your decisions. Anytime you decide to do so, you simply say yes to one opportunity and say no to other possibilities. It can be easy to sit and wonder what-if, but that only leads to frustration. Stop running scenarios in your mind, which will not change what has already happened. Instead of thinking about what may or may not have happened, focus on the present and what you can do now. The past is already gone. Third, decide to let your past go. Once you have expressed your hurt, make a conscious decision to let it go. Although you cannot change your past, you can choose to not dwell on it and take the steps to move on. When you choose to let it go, you take the initiative to move on instead of being a victim to your past. Then forgive yourself and forgive others. You forgive someone for you, not for them. Then you move forward in hope for the future. Stop complaining about what has happened in the past. Do not be a prisoner of your past. If you feel that you must complain to someone, complain to God in prayer, not to your friends and families.

The Spirit of God enlightens us to understand hope. In Ephesians 1:18, Paul says, "I pray that the eyes of your heart may be enlightened in order that you may know the hope to which he has called you, the riches of his glorious inheritance in his holy people."

We learned in the book of James that there are trials we face as we walk with the Lord. We are to consider these trials as an opportunity to experience joy through suffering. James wrote, "Dear brothers and sisters, when troubles come your way, consider it an opportunity for great joy" (James 1:2). So as we walk our walk with Christ, we should not be surprised by these troubles. In fact, the apostle Peter says, "Dear friends, do not be surprised at the fiery trials you are going through, as if something strange were happening to you" (1 Peter 4:12). It is not a matter of *if* we get troubles in our lives; it's a matter of *when* we get them. Jesus warned the disciples about various troubles they would face in life. He said, "I have told you all this so that you may have peace in me. Here on earth you will have many trials and sorrows. But take heart, because I have overcome the world" (John 16:33).

So to help us endure our troubles, God gives us a precious gift in the scriptures. It's called "the psalms of lament." These psalms are the prayers and hymns that God chose to teach us how to express ourselves to Him in worship. They are God's Word and the prayers of men. If you take time to go through these psalms, you will notice about one-third of them are laments. So when you are in trouble, cry out to the Lord. However, do not confuse these rightful laments with the professional complainers who persistently complain about things and never get satisfaction from the Spirit of God. In their prayers, they make statements on the faults of others. Many of them are like children who run to their parents with complaints about their playmates. They whine and because they are angry pour it all out into God's ear and their audience. God wants us to put away childish things and approach him like right-minded and spiritually grown individuals. As the apostle Paul wrote, "When I was a child, I spoke and thought and reasoned as a child. But when I grew up, I put away childish things" (1 Corinthians 13:11). God wants us to complain to Him. However, He does not want us to approach Him like children who complain about their playmates.

In the psalms of lament, the writer pours out to God his sorrow, anger, fear, longing, desolation, repentance, disappointment, and even depression. These are emotions we feel when we experience troubles. God expects us to frequently experience pain and therefore frequently express our pain to Him. He wants us to pour out our complaints to Him and tell Him our troubles. He wants us to do it in three ways. First, He wants us to do it privately like David did when he wrote Psalm 142 in the cave of Adullam (1 Samuel 22). Second, He wants us to do it corporately. The people of Israel sang Psalm 142 together. Third, He wants us to tell Him exactly what it feels like to be in trouble. As David said, "I look for someone to come and help me, but no one gives me a passing thought! No one will help me; no one cares a bit what happens to me (Psalm 142:4). Lastly, God wants us to remember that despite how things look and feel right now, because of His great promises, someday these troubles will no longer afflict us. David said, "Bring me out of prison so that I may give thanks to your name! The righteous will surround me, for you will deal bountifully with me" (Psalm 142:7).

The psalms of lament are a guide for our troubled souls. They truly model for us how to complain to God in ways that bring honor to Him, for they are expressions of God's care and compassion for us. In them, we see that we can complain to God, and we are not alone when our souls are troubled.

Saying the Right Words Is Critical

We often evaluate the quality of someone's prayer by length, wordiness, and eloquence. That is a big Christian mistake. Jesus's prayer is often short, to the point, direct, and brief. Prayer is not about having a certain set of words or a prescribed set of sayings. It is not an incantation or a spell. It is you talking to a friend who is interested in hearing what you have to say. He is the friend who does not care whether your vocabulary is poor or your mispronunciation of some words. You are talking to a kind friend who understands you and is willing to hear you. Prayer is not about making a presentation where everything has to be perfect.

In a presentation, you have to carefully choose your words and tailor them toward your targeted audience. Prayer is about the attitude of your heart. God reads your heart and knows exactly what you are going to say before you even think of it. So don't be overly concerned about what you are going to say or how you are going to say it. Simply begin a conversation with God. Share what's on your mind and your heart with Him. Never let what people say rob you of the prayer life that God wants you to have.

We Should Be in the Right Space to Pray

It is a myth to think you can come before God in prayer only when you get yourself in the right space. We can come to God in any moment, any time, any place, whatever your emotions. Paul was in chains in a Roman prison facing death when he wrote to the Philippians, "Always be full of joy in the Lord. I say it again—rejoice!" (Philippians 4:4). Although Paul was not in a good space, he experienced the joy of the Spirit of God. This joy is not like a happy-go-lucky type of thing where everything is fine. It's a positive emotion we feel when are filled with the Spirit—the deep joy of knowing God is with us in the midst of our troubles. God is in control. If we remember who He is, His promises, and what He can do, we can find a deep joy in our trials and difficult situations.

If Nothing Happens after You Pray, It Means God Said No

Does God truly say no to us after we pray? Sometimes we get discouraged in prayer by thinking God has said no when in fact He's been silent and said nothing at all. Sometimes "Wait" is the answer God gave. Sometimes it's a delay, not a denial. God often delays His answer to cultivate patience and persistence in us and build our faith. Many times, God wants to bring our will around to conform to His own will. This is why praying according to God's will is so critical.

Furthermore, God may say no because He has something far greater in store for us than what we've asked for. In the gospels, we read story of the two sisters, Mary and Martha. When their brother Lazarus was dangerously ill, in desperation they sent for the Lord Jesus because they wanted Him to heal Lazarus, but Jesus had something else in mind. It's the resurrection of Lazarus.

Sometimes God says no to us because in His sovereign will He wants to do something greater for us. I read the story of a carpenter who built crates for the clothes his church wanted to send to an orphanage in China. On his way home, he reached into his shirt pocket to find his glasses, but they were gone. So he drove back to the church and searched for them, but they were nowhere to be found. He replayed his earlier actions in his mind and realized what happened. The glasses had slipped out of his pocket unnoticed and fallen into one of the crates, which he had nailed shut. His brand-new glasses were on their way to China! This was during the Great Depression and money was tight. The man had six children. He had spent $20 for those glasses that morning. In his frustration, the man told God, "It's not fair," as he drove home. "I've been faithful in giving of my time and money to your work, and now this."

Several months later, the director of the orphanage was in the United States. He wanted to visit all the churches that supported him in China, so he came to speak one Sunday night at this small church in Chicago. The carpenter and his family sat in their usual seats in the congregation. The missionary began by thanking the people for their faithfulness in supporting the orphanage. Most of all, he said, "I must thank you for the glasses you sent last year. You see, the Communists had just swept through the orphanage, destroying everything, including my glasses. I was desperate. Even if I had the money, there was simply no way of replacing those glasses. Along with not being able to see well, I experienced headaches every day, so my coworkers and I were much in prayer about this. Then your crates arrived. When my staff removed the covers, they found a pair of glasses lying on top."

The missionary paused long enough to let his words sink in. Then, still gripped with the wonder of it all, he continued. "Folks, when I tried on the glasses, it was as though they had been custom-made for me! I want to thank you for being a part of that." The people listened, happy for the miraculous glasses. However, they thought that the missionary surely must have confused their church with another. There were no glasses on their list of items to be sent overseas.

Sitting quietly in the back, with tears streaming down his face, this carpenter realized the Master Carpenter had used him in an extraordinary way. The will of God is perfect even in our losses. What a great lesson!

Chapter 13

Prayer and Biblical Fasting

Scripture does not command Christians to fast. God does not require or demand it of Christians. However, the Bible presents fasting as something that is good, profitable, and beneficial. We read in the book of Acts that believers fasted before they made important decisions. For instance, it was through worship and fasting that the church at Antioch of Syria commissioned Barnabas and Saul and sent them out as missionaries. Fasting and prayer are often linked together (Luke 2:37; 5:33). The purpose of fasting is to take our eyes off the things of this world to focus completely on God. It is a way to demonstrate to God, and to ourselves, that we are serious about our relationship with Him. Fasting helps us renew our reliance upon God.

Fasting Is a Powerful Spiritual Practice

When Nehemiah's brother arrived from Judah, he broke some sad news to the people in exile about the Israelites living in Jerusalem. He conveyed to them how they were in great trouble. After hearing about it, Nehemiah fasted and prayed to the Lord for days. That's when he discovered that God wanted him to ask the king of Persia for help. He learned that through prayer and fasting. Fasting is a spiritual discipline that helps us center our attention on God and discover His will so we may act according to the will of God. People fast to seek God and know His will. Christians fast in different ways. Some abstain from food while others refrain from various activities such as entertainment, cell phones, social media sites, etc. The period of time one fasts can vary as well. But the focus in each case is to be the same. We fast to seek God and know His will. Fasting is about denying ourselves. We deny ourselves of the things we enjoy the most. When we begin to deny ourselves, several things happen.

First, the Holy Spirit will enable us to set aside earthly matters. For example, relationships, work, and pleasure will take a lesser place in our mind as we concentrate on God and His purposes. Second, our attention will shift from ourselves to God. As a result, our thinking will become clearer, and our ability to understand God's plans will sharpen because we are not distracted by those earthly things. Third, the Lord Jesus, through the Spirit, will certainly do some spiritual cleansing in our lives. His Spirit will convict us of sinful attitudes or behavior. As the apostle John wrote in 1 john 1:9, "If we confess our sins, He is faithful and just to forgive us our sins and to cleanse us from all unrighteousness." So when we get unexpected news like Nehemiah did, we may find our human emotions in turmoil. Nehemiah wisely sought the Lord through fasting and prayer. Fasting is a powerful practice that can help us to hear clearly from God who knows the best way through every situation.

What Biblical Fasting Is Not

Fasting is not saying, "I won't eat food for a day or two." It can be anything you give up temporarily in order to focus all your attention on God, including sexual relations. However, you need to be careful. Some women think they can deprive their husbands of sexual relations because they are fasting and praying. This is biblically wrong. Paul said to the Corinthians,

> Yes, it is good to abstain from sexual relations. But because there is so much sexual immorality, each man should have his own wife, and each woman should have her own husband. The husband should fulfill his wife's sexual needs, and the wife should fulfill her husband's needs. The wife gives authority over her body to her husband, and the husband gives authority over his body to his wife. Do not deprive each other of sexual relations unless you *both agree* to refrain from sexual intimacy for a limited time so you can give yourselves more completely to prayer. Afterward, you should come together again so that Satan won't be able to tempt you because of your lack of self-control. (1 Corinthians 7:1–5)

Fasting should be limited to a set time. It is not intended to punish the flesh but to redirect attention to God. It can be harmful to the body if it's too long, especially if you are diabetic. There are many Christians with diabetes who set aside time to commune with God while abstaining from food, drink, or both. If you are one of those people, can you say with certainty that you fast safely without putting your health at risk? Fasting can impact the health of those with diabetes. Therefore, a diabetic should always consult with their physician before undergoing a fast of any duration. One key factor about fasting with diabetes is whether your diabetes is diet controlled or controlled through medicine. According to some experts, if your diabetes is being controlled strictly through diet and you are not taking medicine to control the symptoms, you should always check with your doctor before fasting if you are under a doctor's care for diabetes.

Biblical Fasting Is Not about Losing Weight

While many people fast to lose weight, dieting is not the purpose of a biblical fast. Christians do not undertake fasting to lose weight but to gain deeper fellowship with God. Many Christians practice the "Daniel Fast" for spiritual victories and deeper fellowship with the Almighty. It is not to lose weight. However, one can physically benefit from it if faithfully practiced. As Susan Gregory wrote, "Fasting is for spiritual purposes, and when using the Daniel Fast, you will benefit physically along with the benefits to your soul and spirit."

Fasting Is Not a Way to Appear More Spiritual than Others

Many Christians fast to show others how spiritual they are. The Pharisees used to fast regularly. One day, the disciples of John the Baptist came to Jesus and asked Him, "Why don't your disciples fast like we do and the Pharisees do?" Jesus replied, "Do wedding guests mourn while celebrating with the groom? Of course not. But someday the groom will be taken away from them, and then they will fast" (Matthew 9:14–15). Jesus told His disciples to not publicize their fast. He said, "And when you fast, don't make it obvious, as the hypocrites do, for they try to look miserable and disheveled so people will admire them for their fasting. I tell you the truth, that is the only reward they will ever get" (Matthew 6:16–18). Fasting is done in a spirit of humility and a joyful attitude.

Reasons to Fast

In the Old Testament, it appears fasting with prayer had to do with a sense of need, dependence, and helplessness in the face of tragedy. The people prayed and fasted in times of mourning, repentance, and deep spiritual need. The prophet Nehemiah prayed and fasted because he was distressed when he learned Jerusalem had been desolated. The wall of Jerusalem was broken, and its gates were burned with fire. The prophet said, "When I heard these things, I sat down and wept. For some days I mourned and fasted and prayed before the God of heaven" (Nehemiah 1:4). Daniel was also devastated at the fall of Jerusalem. "So I turned to the Lord God and pleaded with him in prayer and fasting. I also wore rough burlap and sprinkled myself with ashes" (Daniel 9:3,).

The New Testament does not specifically require believers to fast or set special times for fasting. Jesus does assume we will fast when He says, "And when you fast, don't make it obvious as the hypocrites do" (Matthew 6:16). Note He didn't say if you fast. He says *when* you fast. So Jesus expects believers to fast.

Benefits of Fasting

When we fast, we voluntarily give up on things we love and need temporarily to make room for something more precious—more of God. We exchange food, drink, and water in some cases, things that are vital for our survival for something we need to live, which is more of the presence of God. So fasting increases our sense of humility and dependence on the Lord. It allows us to give more attention to prayer. When we sacrifice some personal comfort to fast and pray, it reminds us that we must daily offer ourselves as a sacrifice to Him. Furthermore, fasting is a good exercise in self-discipline as it strengthens our ability to refrain from sin. It heightens our spiritual and mental alertness and a sense of God's presence as we focus less on the material things of this world and focus more on the heavenly things. Lastly, fasting expresses earnestness and urgency in our prayers.

Prayer and fasting are matters of priorities for the believers. These are priorities in which we have the opportunity to express ourselves to God and give Him an undivided devotion and to the things that concern our spiritual life. This devotion is expressed by abstaining from food and drink, which is a deviation from our normal lives. We do it voluntarily to enjoy a time of uninterrupted communion with God. Prayer and fasting are not a burden or a duty for us. Rather, it is a time we set apart to celebrate God's goodness and mercy to us.

Chapter 14

The Impact of Prayer

Prayer is the lifeblood of an intimate relationship with the Father. Sometimes we have questions about the power and effectiveness of prayer. I want to urge you to not hesitate to take your questions to the Lord, dig into scripture for answers, and seek the counsel of a trusted spiritual mentor. We live in a time of uncertainty. So prayer is too important to neglect. Some Christians seem to have a hard time praying. They spend their days worrying about things and don't have an answer to their problems. They talk to friends and counselors and read books trying to find help on their own. Some listen to specific radio broadcasts, podcasts, and so forth. They engage in such endeavors to avoid getting on their knees before God. But the Word of God is clear that we are to go to Him first. The Lord Jesus said, "Seek first the kingdom of God and His righteousness, and all these things shall be added to you" (Matthew 6:33). David said in Psalm 138, "In the day when I cried out, You answered me, and made me bold with strength in my soul" (Psalm 138:3). In all his trials, he turned to no one else but God. God answered him and gave him strength for the battle he was facing.

God's promises given to us are evident in His Word. But when it comes to prayer, God in His Word gives us more than promises; it also gives us warnings about the danger we face when we neglect prayer. It says in the book of Hebrews, "How shall we escape if we neglect so great a salvation" (Hebrews 2:3). In the Greek language, it means "taking something lightly." Since the author in this context is discussing things related to salvation, it appears that prayer is one of the subjects of discussion. We face all kinds of problems when we neglect our prayer life. We often hear God's voice speaking to us through His Word. So in our dark days as when we pray, He will hear us. In this life, we are under constant attack from devil, facing trouble and temptations on all sides. Therefore, it is necessary if we want to be victorious to seek God constantly. What is important is that you change your priorities. You find time to do everything else in your daily routine. If you find time to visit with friends, washing your car, shopping, dining out, watching sports, and so forth, you can make time to pray. And that will make a positive impact on your life. Your life would be so much richer and more effective in every way if you would put Jesus at the very top of your daily routine.

Will God's Plans for Your Life Fail if You Do not Pray?

First of all, let me say that God is not subservient to us or dependent upon our prayers. As we serve the Lord, we invest our time in the work He called us to accomplish for His glory. The time we invest in speaking with Him involves us in the work that He is doing in our lives and in the world. But He will execute His plan without us. It is important to understand that laboring alongside the Lord is a privilege. So does my prayer (or lack thereof) impact God's work? Scripture indicates the answer to this question is both yes and no, depending upon the situation. There are times when God's purpose is set. He is in control and has determined the best course of action. In the Old Testament, the Lord often prophesied what He would do and then brought those events to pass. In other cases, He doesn't. He expects us to ask. James

4:2 says, "You do not have because you do not ask" (James 4:2). There are some good things that He holds back until we go to Him in prayer to receive them. However, you need to remember that God is a loving Father. So in His love, He pours His blessings upon us that we would not even think to request.

Our prayers have a tremendous impact, particularly on our own faith and life. It is a formidable privilege to kneel before the all-powerful Father and know that He listens and will respond. God loves His children, and He is good enough to answer their prayers.

Prayer in Times of Failure

The biggest tool of Satan to diminish the believer's faith is the fear of failure. Sometimes, he uses other people to discourage us from moving forward. But we cannot serve God and be constantly worried about what other people think. We have to move forward. Scripture says in the book of Proverbs, "Fear of man will prove to be a snare, but whoever trusts in the Lord is kept safe" (Proverbs 29:25 NIV). So to move forward, one must get rid of the fear of failure. Some of us are afraid of failure and that prevents us from acting and move forward with a goal. Failure is not failing to reach your goal. Failure is not failing to hit your intended target. You think that you failed in your endeavor because you did not reach that target. Failure is not any of those. Failure is when you stop trying. Failure is not falling down. Failure is when you fall down and refuse to get back up. No one is ever a failure until he or she quits. So if you're attempting something for God, it is worth pursuing the endeavor because it's a good thing. Failure is not trying and not accomplishing anything. Failure is failing to try.

You can get rid of the fear of failure in a variety of ways. One is to never compare yourself to someone else. One thing you need to realize is that there is always going to be someone who's doing a better job than you. That is always the case. That may get you discouraged when you realize that, and don't become prideful. Discouragement and pride are two obstacles that will certainly keep you from serving

God as He intends for you to be in your walk with Him. The apostle Paul in his letter to the Galatians wrote, "Each one should test their own actions. Then they can take pride in themselves alone, without comparing themselves to someone else" (Galatians 6:4 NIV). You may a legitimate reason to be proud. It is being prideful that is sinful. So you might say that there's a good kind of pride and a bad kind of pride. The bad kind of pride is when you compare yourself to someone else when you say, "I'm better than so and so!" The good kind of pride is when you say, "God, I'm proud of what You're doing in my life, my family, my walk with You." That's the good kind of pride. And I believe we all should have that kind of pride.

God is never in the comparison business. We should not do that either. When we get to heaven, God isn't going to ask you, "Why weren't you more like so and so?" He's going to say, "Why weren't you like My Son, Jesus? Or why weren't you who I made you to be?" Think about that!

The fear of failure is something you need to get rid of because it will prevent you from doing what God called you to do for His glory. Anything we are attempting for God in faith is a good thing, regardless of the results. Someone else may have a better result doing the same thing. But that is not a reason for you to fear moving forward. Let God be the judge of that. Satan wants to use our fears to hold us back from living boldly for God. As believers, we must live in faith. Therefore, we need to pray to God asking Him to give us boldness to live confidently as we pursue the work He called us to accomplish for His glory.

Sometimes, we may feel a sense of inadequacy as we approach the Lord in prayer for some pressing needs. Nehemiah seemed to have had such time when God put in his heart a burning desire to go to Jerusalem. After the Jews had returned from exile to Jerusalem, the prophet Nehemiah's heart was burdened by a desire to help. God put that desire in his heart. We can imagine a sense of inadequacy that may have engulfed the prophet since he was not in Jerusalem. He was far away in exile serving a Babylonian king. But God got his attention. As a servant of the king, Nehemiah didn't have the freedom to pack up and leave. But internally, he was hard-pressed to return to Jerusalem.

Whenever God puts a burden on our hearts, He will open a door to accomplish His will. In this case, the Lord used Nehemiah's desperate prayer to prepare a pagan king to send him on his mission.

Since the Lord is calling us to a task that seems beyond our abilities, we may feel inadequate and list a bunch of reasons to justify that we cannot do it. If you feel that way, let me tell you that God already knows everything about you and the situation. The thing is God is not asking your permission to proceed; rather, He is calling you to move forward with faith and obedience. He did not make a mistake in choosing you for the task, but you will make a huge one if you refuse to do it. God always equips the one He calls for the task at hand. Because the Holy Spirit dwells within every believer, we have all we need to fulfill our Lord's mission. Instead of letting inadequacy hinder you from obeying, let it drive you to your knees so you can arise with renewed insight and power.

The Undesired Effects of Fear

Fear is a human emotion that protects us from danger. It is an unavoidable facet of the human experience. People consider fear an unpleasant emotion. In an article entitled "Dissecting Terror: How Does Fear Work?" published by *Medical News Today,* researchers who study fear say that biologically, what happens in our bodies when we are scared sometimes gets out of control.

People often refer to the physiological changes that occur when a person experiences fear as the fight-or-flight response. This means when a person is afraid, he or she either fights what causes the fear or flees from it. When we are afraid, our breathing rate increases, our heart rate is faster, the central blood vessels around vital organs dilate to flood them with oxygen and nutrients, and muscles are pumped with blood, ready to react. The experts continue to say that metabolically, levels of glucose in the blood spike, providing a ready store of energy if the need for action arises. Similarly, levels of calcium and white blood cells in the bloodstream see an increase.

Obviously, fear produces anxiety, but it also creates chaos in our lives and even affects those around us. The effects of fear can be devastating to our lives. It may somehow suppress our thinking and actions. In ministry, fear can create indecisiveness that results in stagnation. Some of us are very talented; however, we procrastinate indefinitely rather than taking a risk because of the fear of failure.

Fear hinders us from becoming the people God wants us to be. As people of God, when we are dominated by negative emotions, we cannot fulfill our purpose and achieve the goals He has in mind for us. A lack of self-confidence hinders our belief in what the Lord can do with our lives. Fear can steal our peace and contentment. When a person is always afraid, their life becomes centered on pessimism and therefore creates doubt. God promises us an abundant life, but if we surrender to the chains of fear, our prayers will not avail much.

Are you afraid of loss, rejection, or death? Let me remind you that all of us will face such realities at some point in our lives. All you need to know is God will never reject you, even though some people will. But He will always be on your side. The Bible tells us that God will meet all our needs. Read what Jesus said to His disciples.

> Therefore I tell you, do not be anxious about your life, what you will eat, nor about your body, what you will put on. For life is more than food, and the body more than clothing. Consider the ravens: they neither sow nor reap, they have neither storehouse nor barn, and yet God feeds them. Of how much more value are you than the birds! And which of you by being anxious can add a single hour to his span of life? If then you are not able to do as small a thing as that, why are you anxious about the rest? Consider the lilies, how they grow: they neither toil nor spin, yet I tell you, even Solomon in all his glory was not arrayed like one of these. (Matthew 6:25–33 ESV)

So our only concern is to obey the Heavenly Father and leave the consequences to Him.

Chapter 15

Praying for Change

The world is constantly changing. We have seen many dynamic changes in the few years. Some good, some bad. The pandemic has created a lot of changes in our way of life. We are forced to live a certain way to protect ourselves, family, and neighbors. Maintaining faith, courage, and energy in today's world is not easy. People slowly lose hope and begin to feel trapped by the circumstances of life. Some have even committed suicide. This is certainly due to unwanted and unwelcome changes that occur because of the world phenomena.

The changes caused by the pandemic generated a global crisis. There are economic uncertainties as markets rise and fall, employment fluctuates, and conflicts erupt among people of all ethnicities. The world is in turmoil and countries have been going through troubles never seen before. People are continuously faced with events outside of their control. As time passes, it seems like the future takes on greater uncertainty. In the midst of chaos and turmoil, and society unrest, God offers us something that the world cannot give us, and that is His peace. His peace surpasses all human understanding. The scripture says, "Peace I leave with you; my peace I give you. I do not give to you as the world gives. Do not let your hearts be troubled and do not be afraid" (John 14:27). Thomas Holdcroft said, "There may be those on earth who dress better or eat better, but those who enjoy the peace of God sleep better."

In times of crisis, we need to anchor our hope on God. Because it is a change and will end someday. In this life where things are constantly changing, I invite you to be anchored to the things that never change. Your schedule has changed, your life has changed, your groceries needs have changed, your travel arrangements have changed, and your work habits have changed. Everything is changing and that has been hard on everyone. However, I want to encourage you to anchor your souls to the things that have not changed. Scripture says that God never changes. Anchor your soul to the God of hope who "will fill you with peace, joy, and assurance" for the future.

Dealing with changes in this life is hard. It is hard to really walk in faith and not by sight. It is hard to remain faithful when you do not know where your journey will take you. But the Word of God declares that He will instruct you and teach you in the way you should go. Even though the path ahead is uncertain and unfamiliar, God will counsel you through His Spirit. As the world changes, all you need to do is ask God to change things in your favor. Prayer changes things. Scripture says in 1 John, "This is the confidence we have in approaching God: that if we ask anything according to his will, he hears us" (1 John 5:14).

So anything we pray for that aligns with God's will and plan for your life will be granted. The more time we spend with God, the more we'll come to understand His will and how to pray for it. It is important to remember that prayer doesn't change God's mind, but it does transform the believer's heart.

Some of our requests may be granted immediately simply because we asked with the realization that God loves to give us good gifts. Other requests may require time before they can be given. Meanwhile, we must simply be diligent to persevere in prayer. Whatever the Lord's response or timing, we trust that He has only the best in store for His children. That means we might not receive exactly what we have asked Him for, but He will give us something even better. For instance, His immense pleasure, because God alone perfectly knows our heart's desire and wishes to fulfill it. Prayer lets us witness God's hand in any situation. And as we give attention, time, and perseverance in prayer, we will find no limit to what He can achieve in our hearts and circumstances.

Chapter 16

Praying the Promises of God

In this chapter, I want to focus on the promises of God. As you know, the Bible is the actual Word of God Almighty. It is truth. And I mentioned in the previous chapter, God never changes. Therefore, His Word never changes. The Word of God enables us in all circumstances, so we have a sure foundation on which to base our lives and decisions. Jesus said that we would endure hardship in this life. But God gave His children amazing tools to keep trials from overwhelming us. For instance, He placed His Spirit inside each believer to guide and empower. Furthermore, He gave us prayer so we could not only communicate and stay connected with our Him but also bring Him our requests.

There are thousands of promises in scripture. God promised to bless Abraham and, through his descendants, the entire world. This promise, called the Abrahamic Covenant, pointed to the coming Messiah, the Lord Jesus (John 8:56). God promised Israel to be their God and make them His people. God promised that if we search for Him, we will find Him (Deuteronomy 4:29). It says in Deuteronomy, "Our God is near us whenever we pray to him" (Deuteronomy 4:7). God promised protection for His children (Psalm 121). God promised salvation to all who believe in His Son (Romans 1:16–17). There is no greater blessing than the gift of God's salvation that we freely received.

He promised that all things will work out for good for His children (Romans 8:28). This keeps us from being discouraged by present circumstances.

God promised comfort in our trials (2 Corinthians 1:3–4). He has a plan, and one day we will be able to share the comfort we receive. God promised every spiritual blessing in Christ (Ephesians 1:3). In the Old Testament, God had promised physical blessing to Israel. But to the church today He has promised spiritual blessings "in the heavenly places." God promised to finish the work He started in us (Philippians 1:6). God does nothing in half measures. He started the work in us, and He will be sure to complete it.

God promised peace when we pray (Philippians 4:6–7). His peace is protection. It will "guard your hearts and your minds in Christ." God promised to supply our needs (Matthew 6:33; Philippians 4:19). Not that we get everything we want, but our needs will be taken care of. Following Jesus brings us more spiritual fulfillment than we could have anticipated. Jesus promised eternal life to those who trust Him (John 4:14). The Good Shepherd also promised to hold us securely. "No one will snatch them out of my hand" (John 10:28).

There are many more promises of God in scripture. All of them find their ultimate fulfillment in Jesus Christ, "the radiance of God's glory" (Hebrews 1:3). God's promises are yes in Christ. Paul told the Corinthians, "For no matter how many promises God has made, they are 'Yes' in Christ. And so, through him the 'Amen' is spoken by us to the glory of God" (2 Corinthians 1:20). These promises are true, and we count on them.

We have assurances that we can rely on with perfect confidence. And they are limitless. God wants us to learn these assurances so we will not miss His blessings. We need to turn His promises into prayers and to cry out to Him to bless our hearts. Sometimes we have to make difficult decisions. We need God's counsel to guide us as make these decisions. Psalm 32:8 states, "I will instruct you and teach you in the way which you should go; I will counsel you with My eye upon you." As we pray, we can pray God's words back to Him, saying that we believe He will teach us and reveal His path while remaining by our side as our caregiver through the entire situation. We face adversities quite often in our daily lives. When difficulties arise, we need a solid foundation on which to stand. Otherwise, our emotions could easily lead us astray through faulty thinking. We need to remember that God is faithful and unchanging so we can trust in His promises that enable us to rest confidently and act boldly.

It is up to us to make a choice to not worry about the things of this life, for our God is a God of peace and understanding who is able to help us to deal with the changes that are happening in our lives. He made this promise in His Word. Scripture says to

> not be anxious about anything, but in everything by prayer and supplication with thanksgiving let your requests be made known to God. And the peace of God, which surpasses all understanding, will guard your hearts and your minds in Christ Jesus. Finally, brothers, whatever is true, whatever is honorable, whatever is just, whatever is pure, whatever is lovely, whatever is commendable, if there is any excellence, if there is anything worthy of praise, think about these things. (Philippians 4:6–8)

The devil uses our tough times to try to distance us from God. But we know that nothing can separate us from the love of God. Not hard times, not heights, not depths. Nothing, because He is the God of love. He is with you always and will never forsake you. You may feel weary at times, but His grace and strength will keep you going. Our Lord Jesus is a shoulder we can lean on during our difficult situations. He promised to take you yoke upon Himself. In Him, you can certainly find peace. Rest your heart rests in Him.

God promised to be with us always, but He did not promise us the absence of troubles. In fact, the Lord said, "I have said these things to you, that in me you may have peace. In the world you will have tribulation. But take heart; I have overcome the world" (John 6:33). He promised to be with us when calamities strike. We need to count on His promise during the seasons of hardships. He will give you wisdom and strength to overcome all these difficulties. As you pray, ask Him to deliver you from the discouraging times and let your trust be in Him alone. The Lord has made these promises and will not violate any of them, for He is a faithful God who keeps all His promises.

Chapter 17

My Prayers for You

I don't know about you, but sometimes when I pray, I feel like I'm playing a sport with my eyes closed not knowing if I'm going to make the basket or hit the goal. You throw some words heavenward and wonder if they've reached heaven because there is no obvious progress. You pray and hope something happens. I believe when we pray, our words reach heaven and God listens. But we don't want our words to just touch heaven, but we want them to move heaven's power on our behalf. We want to pray knowing that our words are not just heard but come back down with God's clear answers. In other words, we want the Lord's will to fall on earth, not because we are good but because He is good and does things according to His own purpose, His will, and our good. We need to understand and believe that God is always good.

God's power is held within His Word. There are numerous prayers in scripture that we can use to bless our soul.

Thanking God for You

In my prayer for those God put in paths, those who will read this book—and I consider you one—I pray that God fill you with the knowledge of His will, wisdom, and understanding so that you may understand and accept His will. I ask God to help you pursue others with love, through prayer, while building unity in your congregations and/or groups where you belong.

Paul prayed for the Philippian believers in this manner: "I thank my God in all my remembrance of you, always in every prayer of mine for you all making my prayer with joy, because of your partnership in the gospel from the first day until now. And I am sure of this, that he who began a good work in you will bring it to completion at the day of Jesus Christ." (Philippians 1:3–6 ESV). For the Romans, he prayed, "First, I thank my God through Jesus Christ for all of you, because your faith is proclaimed in all the world. For God is my witness, whom I serve with my spirit in the gospel of his Son, that without ceasing I mention you always in my prayers, asking that somehow by God's I will now at last succeed in coming to you" (Romans 1:8–10 ESV).

Praying for Others to Be Saved

If you are not a believer and just happen to read this book, I pray that God helps you to understand the fullness of his love. The scripture says in Romans 10:1, "Brothers, my heart's desire and prayer to God for them is that they may be saved" (Romans 10:1). Also, in Philemon 5–7, the scripture says, "Because I hear about your love for all his holy people and your faith in the Lord Jesus. I pray that your partnership with us in the faith may be effective in deepening your understanding of every good thing we share for the sake of Christ. Your love has given me great joy and encouragement, because you, brother, have refreshed the hearts of the Lord's people."

May God Encourage Your Heart

I pray that the power of Jesus Christ continually fills your heart with joy, grace, peace, and hope through the Holy Spirit. May the God of hope fill you with all joy and peace as you trust in Him so that you may overflow with hope by the power of the Holy Spirit (Romans 15:13). I pray that the grace of the Lord Jesus be with you (1 Corinthians 16:23). As Paul prayed for the Colossian church, I pray and ask that you may be filled with the knowledge of God's will in all spiritual wisdom and understanding so as to walk in a manner worthy of the Lord, fully pleasing to Him: bearing fruit in every good work and increasing in the knowledge of God; being strengthened with all power, according to His glorious might, for all endurance and patience with joy; and giving thanks to the Father, who has qualified you to share in the inheritance of the saints in light. He has delivered us from the domain of darkness and transferred us to the kingdom of His beloved Son in whom we have redemption, the forgiveness of sins (Colossians 1:9–14). May all blessings be passed on to you as your read these words.

May Your Heart Be in Prayer Continually

The apostle Paul, while in chains, prayed wholeheartedly the for the Colossian church. I want to use his words to pray for you as did Paul. I pray that God brightens your ways, opens doors to you, and gives you a word for others to hear. May the mysteries of Lord Jesus Christ be open as you fearlessly convey His Word. I pray that you devote yourself to prayer, being watchful and thankful. And pray for other believers, too, that God may open a door for the message of the Bible given to us so that we may proclaim the mystery of Christ.

Pray that the gospel may be proclaimed clearly, as it should. To the church in Rome Paul wrote, "I appeal to you, brothers, by our Lord Jesus Christ and by the love of the Spirit, to strive together with me in your prayers to God on my behalf" (Romans 15:30). Today, I pray that you may be rescued from your struggle so that by God's will, you may come to fully enjoy the work you are called to. May the God of peace be with you!

Offer Praises to God's Name in Your Prayers

We must acknowledge the goodness of God. We must praise Him for who He is, what He does for us, and how we've been blessed in His Son, Christ Jesus.

Paul prayed that the Corinthians would understand that we must praise God, who comforts us when we are going through difficult times. He wrote,

> Blessed be the God and Father of our Lord Jesus Christ, the Father of mercies and God of all comfort, who comforts us in all our affliction, so that we may be able to comfort those who are in any affliction, with the comfort with which we ourselves are comforted by God. For as we share abundantly in Christ's sufferings, so through Christ we share abundantly in comfort too. If we are afflicted, it is for your comfort and salvation; and if we are comforted, it is for your comfort, which you experience when you patiently endure the same sufferings that we suffer. Our hope for you is unshaken, for we know that as you share in our sufferings, you will also share in our comfort. (2 Corinthians 1:3–7)

He prays the same way for the Christians in the Ephesian church.

> Praise be to the God and Father of our Lord Jesus Christ, who has blessed us in the heavenly realms with every spiritual blessing in Christ. For he chose us in him before the creation of the world to be holy and blameless in his sight. In love he predestined us to be adopted as his sons through Jesus Christ, in accordance with his pleasure and will—to the praise of his glorious grace, which he has freely given us in the One he loves. In him we have redemption through his blood, the forgiveness of sins, in accordance with the riches of God's grace that

he lavished on us with all wisdom and understanding. (Ephesians 1:3)

Prayer of Thanksgiving to God for Fellow Believers

Remember to offer praises to God in things. He is the one who does all things. He is the one who brings life and delivers hope to us. We must thank the Lord you for enriching our lives, keeping us, and equipping us with spiritual blessings. God supplies our needs, and we lack nothing. We must praise Him. Paul gives us reasons to thank God in his letter to the Corinthians.

> But thanks be to God, who in Christ always leads us in triumphal procession, and through us spreads the fragrance of the knowledge of him everywhere. For we are the aroma of Christ to God among those who are being saved and among those who are perishing, to one a fragrance from death to death, to the other a fragrance from life to life. Who is sufficient for these things? (2 Corinthians 2:14–16).

Like Paul, we must thank God for our fellow believers, those in put in our paths. Paul wrote,

> I always thank God for you because of his grace given you in Christ Jesus. For in him you have been enriched in every way—in all your speaking and in all your knowledge—because our testimony about Christ was confirmed in you. Therefore, you do not lack any spiritual gift as you eagerly wait for our Lord Jesus Christ to be revealed. He will keep you strong to the end, so that you will be blameless on the day of our Lord Jesus Christ. God, who has called you into fellowship with his Son Jesus Christ our Lord, is faithful. (1 Corinthians 1:4–9)

A Prayer of Healing for You

I do not claim to have the gift of healing, I believe that Jesus is the Great Healer. He can heal you if you pray according to His will. No prayer is effectual apart from God's will. In times of trouble, sickness, distress, or heartache for whatever reason, you can find a comforting message from God. God is always there for you. As the psalmist said, "The Lord is near to the brokenhearted and saves the crushed in spirit" (Psalm 34:18). Therefore, I pray that God blesses you with His loving care. May He renew your strength and heal whatever troubles you. Going through a period of suffering can be unnerving and frustrating. Whether you're overcoming an illness or injury or mourning the loss of a loved one, you can sometimes feel stuck, but know that God is there even in the middle of your pain. Let me remind you that in times like these, you are not alone. You may not foresee a finite timeline for recovery, but God, who controls times and circumstances, will be there with you along the way whether it is emotional, spiritual, or physical pain.

However, if you do not see healing, please understand the truth of God's Word. May you know that all God gives is more than enough and that, in you, the Lord is still working. Accept the will of God. The great apostle Paul said, "Three times I pleaded with the Lord to take (thorn in flesh) away from me. But he said to me, 'My grace is sufficient for you, for my power is made perfect in weakness'" (2 Corinthians 12: 8–9). As the psalmist said, "My flesh and my heart may fail, but God is the strength of my heart and my portion forever" (Psalm 73:26).

A Prayer for Your Sanctification

May the Lord sanctify you more and more. Paul prayed for the Philippians so that their love for Christ may abound more and more. He wrote, "And it is my prayer that your love may abound more and more, with knowledge and all discernment, so that you may approve what is excellent, and so be pure and blameless for the day of Christ, filled with the fruit of righteousness that comes through Jesus Christ, to the glory and praise of God" (Philippians 1:9–11 ESV). Not to be too technical here, which is not the goal of this book, but I assume that positionally you are sanctified. What I mean by that is that your positional sanctification is your actual state before the Lord. It means that when you were saved you were sanctified. At the time of your salvation, you were set apart from the devil unto God, from darkness unto light, and from death unto life. By God's grace, you were set apart from hell unto heaven, from the destruction of sin to the dominion of God and His glory. That part of sanction occurred when you were saved.

Furthermore, you received a new nature. As Paul puts it, "The old has passed away; behold, the new has come" (2 Corinthians 5:17). Now you have the life of Christ within you. And this the holy life that resides in you through the indwelling of Holy Spirit has taken up residence in you. You can say that you have the holy life of God within you. That's your sanctification. Because of this privilege, you now love what is right and hate what is wrong. You find yourself desiring to obey the will of God and His Word. That is the work of the Spirit in you. The Spirit of God gives you a new standing in Christ, which is your new nature. God covers you with the robe of Christ's righteousness so that when He sees you, He sees you as righteous in Christ. As the prophet Isaiah said, "You have the robe of righteousness." Isaiah wrote, "I will greatly rejoice in the Lord; my soul shall exult in my God, for he has clothed me with the garments of salvation; he has covered me with the robe of righteousness." (You have the robe of righteousness.) So you are now in Christ. He was made sin on the cross, that you might become the righteousness of God in Him. You can say that you bear the very righteousness of Christ. You are therefore declared righteous.

In Christ, you are declared holy, and you are set apart unto holiness. That is why a believer can be called a holy one. It is God who declared you holy. Sometimes believers are called "saints." It is the same word translated *holy*. You are a saint and precious in the sight of God. When Paul wrote to the Romans, he said, "To all those in Rome who are loved by God and called to be saints" (Romans 1:7). Also, when Paul wrote to the Corinthians, he called them saints. Sanctified. He said sanctified saints. That is what was achieved through Christ's provision on the cross: the positional reality of those who believe. You are part of a sanctified body.

Another aspect of our holiness and sanctification is that God Himself sanctifies His people. Praying that God blesses the Thessalonians, Paul wrote, "Now may the God of peace Himself sanctify you entirely; and may your spirit and soul and body be preserved complete, without blame at the coming of our Lord Jesus Christ' (1 Thessalonians 5:23). God is the one who brought the sanctifying process all bound up in the saving work. In fact, only He can provide the kind of holiness He requires from us. Jesus in John 17:17 said, "Sanctify them in the truth; your word is truth." So you can understand that if God is going to sanctify us, He's going to do it through His Word. The apostle Peter says, "And after you have suffered a little while, the God of all grace, who has called you to his eternal glory in Christ, will himself restore, confirm, strengthen, and establish you" (1 Peter 5:10). You see, God uses sufferings and trials to sanctify us. It is obvious that this is the way He perfects, strengthens, and establishes those who believe.

A third aspect of our sanctification to understand is the ultimate sanctification. This is the future aspect. Positional sanctification is something that has already happened. The ultimate sanctification will happen in the future. This aspect of our sanctification will be established at our glorification. The first aspect was established at our justification when we were saved. This one will be at our glorification. At the moment when we leave this world to be in the presence of God, we enter ultimate sanctification. At that moment, we lose this vile flesh, which give us problems of all sorts, and this fallen humanness: our body, soul, and spirit. In every part, we will be absolutely sanctified. Just as Paul told the Corinthians, "In a moment, in the twinkling of an eye, at the last trumpet. For the trumpet will sound, and the dead will be raised imperishable, and we shall be changed. For this perishable body must put on the imperishable, and this mortal body must put on immortality. When the perishable puts on the imperishable, and the mortal puts on immortality" (1 Corinthians 15:52–54). That is when the Lord will transform our actual body into the body of His glory. When that happens, we will become like Christ for we see Him as He is. At that glorious moment, we will be presented as a bride without spot and without blemish, glorious in holiness, to our bridegroom. That is our future and ultimate sanctification.

As Paul prayed for the holiness of the Corinthians, I hope this prayer will also apply to your life. "But we pray to God that you may not do wrong—not that we may appear to have met the test, but that you may do what is right, though we may seem to have failed. For we cannot do anything against the truth, but only for the truth. For we are glad when we are weak, and you are strong. Your restoration is what we pray for" (2 Corinthians 13:7–9).

A Prayer for God's Protection

We live in a dangerous world. Though evil and danger are everywhere, we have a God that loves us and promises to protect us. Therefore, we can rest assured that God will care for us and keep us safe. Let's remember that our God is faithful. Paul told the Thessalonians, "But the Lord is faithful. He will establish you and guard you against the evil one" (2 Thessalonians 3:3). The prophet Isaiah said, "Fear not, for I am with you; be not dismayed, for I am your God; I will strengthen you, I will help you, I will uphold you with my righteous right hand" (Isaiah 41:10).

We face danger and fear every day. I pray that God always keep you in the shadow of His wing. When life is hard and you don't know what to do, may God help you remember that He is always with you and that you are never alone. As children of God, we cannot live without Him.

Remember the promise of God's continual presence. I encourage you to keep on walking and live under the protection of God Almighty. The psalmist said, "He who dwells in the shelter of the Most High will abide in the shadow of the Almighty. I will say to the Lord, "My refuge and my fortress, my God, in whom I trust." For he will deliver you from the snare of the fowler and from the deadly pestilence. He will cover you with his pinions, and under his wings you will find refuge; his faithfulness is a shield and buckler" (Psalm 91:1–4). So I encourage you to be strong and courageous as your face your difficulties. God promised us to be with us as we face danger and the attack of the enemy. God told Moses, who later relayed the message to his successor, Joshua, "Be strong and courageous, for you shall go with this people into the land that the Lord has sworn to their fathers to give them, and you shall put them in possession of it. It is the Lord who goes before you. He will be with you; he will not leave you or forsake you. Do not fear or be dismayed" (Deuteronomy 31:7–8).

I pray for your protection and the presence of God to be manifest in your life where you may be, whatever you may be doing. I thank the Lord for protecting you. I thank Him for the angels that He assigns to watch over you. Be at peace, my dear brethren, knowing that your life is in God's hands.

Amen.

Bibliography

Blackaby, T. C. (2008). *Fresh Encounter: Experiencing God through Prayer, Humility, and a Heartfelt Desire to Know Him.* B&H Publishing Group.

Gregory, S. (2008). *The Daniel Cure: The Daniel Fast Way to Vibrant Health.*

Exantus, W. R. (2012). *Pastoral Burnout & Leadership Styles: Factors Contributing to Stress and Ministerial Turnover.* Bloomington, IN: Author House Publishing.

Holy Bible, New International Version, copyright © 1973, 1978, 1984, 2011 by Biblica, Inc.

Holy Bible, New Living Translation, copyright ©1996, 2004, 2007. Tyndale House Publishers, Inc., Carol Stream, Illinois.

The ESV Bible (The Holy Bible, English Standard Version), copyright © 2001 by Crossway Bibles, a publishing ministry of Good News Publishers.

New American Standard Bible, copyright © 1960, 1962, 1963, 1968, 1971, 1972, 1973, 1975, 1977, 1995 by the Lockman Foundation, La Habra, California.

Voltaire (François-Marie Arouet). "Vie de Voltaire" of his visitors at Ferney given by Duvernet, 1798.

https://danielfast.wordpress.com/2008/06/27/daniel-fast-and-weight-loss/.

http://www.cbsnews.com/news/funeral-for-former-haitian-dictator-draws-hundreds/.

http://www.huffingtonpost.com/2012/11/14/tammi-estep-stabbing-south-carolina_n_2130765.html.

Matthew, S. "Mattie Stepanek, 13, Poet and Inspiration." *New York Times.* June 23, 2004. Retrieved July 20, 2022.

https://www.medicalnewstoday.com/articles/323492.

From the Same Author

Pastoral Burnout and Leadership Styles: Factors Contributing to Stress and Ministerial Turnover

Effectual Prayers: Seven ways to praying according to God's will

How to Develop Your Prayer Life

We need a consistent prayer life to experience victories in the Lord. It is essential to those who serve in the ministry. It's a lifestyle of prayer that should be developed in order to receive the fullness of what God has provided for us. It's a commitment that we need to make to seek to spend time in prayer with God daily. Spending time with God daily will help us develop a strong prayer life. Here are three simple ways believers can develop a prayer life.

1. Set a schedule for regular prayer times.

Having a schedule helps establish when during the day we will pray. Most Christians pray more by simply developing a schedule for regular prayer times. There are many who love God dearly but never develop a consistent prayer life. The reason is simple: a lack of discipline in prayer. We all have busy days. There will be days when you will fail to comply with your normal schedule, but you can always make adjustments. Once your prayer time has been scheduled, we must do our best to faithfully comply with it. It is now considered sacred time set apart with God; it is a divine appointment, not legalistic as some might say. You're being faithful and consistent in your time with God. You should consider this time sacred; you miss it only in case of an emergency.

2. Make a prayer list.

A prayer list helps us to focus on what to pray for. Developing a prayer list is, in part, being systematic in our prayers. However, it is helpful to understand that there are times when this may change due to God's power and favor being released while we pray. Our prayer list is an essential tool that helps us focus on things important to God and us. Again, it's praying according to God's will. A prayer list might include family members, ministry leaders, ministries, friends, persons in authority (1 Timothy 2:2), and so forth. You may deviate from your prayer list or omit parts of it as the Spirit of God leads.

3. Have a right view of God.

A right view of God causes us to want to pray. A successful life of prayer depends a lot on a right view of God. Many Christians have a wrong view of God. If our view of God is wrong, it is certain we're not going to have a successful prayer life. Some of us see God as a taskmaster who forces His followers to engage in conversation with Him through prayer to receive our tasks from Him in order to prove our devotion to Him. To the contrary, God is a tender loving Father who listens to us and wants to develop a loving relationship with us as His children.

If we seek God with all our heart through His Son, Jesus, He will energize our spirit to understand Him and trust Him as a child trusts his father. This is foundational to a growing prayer life. Before our Lord Jesus was arrested and betrayed to be crucified, He prayed to His Father for us. Jesus said, "I am in them, and you are in me. May they experience such perfect unity that the world will know that you sent me and that you love them as much as you love me" (John 17:23). Our Lord gave us great worth. So because of what Jesus said, we have confidence that God enjoys us even in our weaknesses. God is a tender and merciful God who is gentle with our weakness after we repent. Paul says in Romans, "You received God's Spirit when He adopted you as His own children. Now we call Him, Abba, Father" (Romans 8:15). We call our human father "Papa" because we him as our father and he knows us his sons and daughters. Likewise, our Father in heaven knows us as His children through His own Son, Jesus.

Understanding Jesus as the Son of God, our Savior and Lord, His Spirit as our guide gives us a vibrant prayer life. Jesus has a heart filled with gladness and affections for us. So as sons of God in Jesus, we are in the position to experience God's throne as heirs of His power. Paul said to the Romans, "And since we are his children, we are his heirs. In fact, together with Christ, we are heirs of God's glory. But if we are to share his glory, we must also share his suffering" (Romans 8:17). A right view of God is to see Him as our Father and His Son as our mediator through whom all intercessions to the Father are made in fellowship with Holy Spirit. The presence of the Holy Spirit in our hearts connects us with God the Father. Apart from connecting with God through the Spirit, we can do nothing that effectively renews our love and releases His revelation and power in our heart.

Printed in the United States
by Baker & Taylor Publisher Services